OREGON TERRITORY:

CONTAINING

A BRIEF, BUT AUTHENTIC ACCOUNT

OF

SPANISH, ENGLISH, RUSSIAN, AND AMERICAN

DISCOVERIES

ON THE

NORTH-WEST COAST OF AMERICA.

ALSO,

THE DIFFERENT TREATY STIPULATIONS CONFIRMING THE
CLAIM OF THE

UNITED STATES,

AND OVERLAND EXPEDITIONS TO THE COLUMBIA RIVER,

WITH INCIDENTS OF

PERIL AND ADVENTURE

CONNECTED WITH THEIR HISTORY, &c. &c.

BY H. L. W. LEONARD, ESQ.

CLEVELAND:
YOUNGLOVE'S STEAM PRESS.
1846.

HISTORY *of* THE OREGON TERRITORY

NOTES

The Leonard history of the Oregon Territory is one of the rarest books pertaining to the history of the American west.

About 1928 or 1929 a copy of the Leonard history held by Goodspeeds, Boston, was acquired by the Edward Eberstadt Company of New York and this was sold to the Coe Collection, Yale University. A second copy turned up in 1928 and was sold by Eberstadt to Thomas W. Streeter of New Jersey. Following Mr. Streeter's death this copy was sold at auction to an unknown buyer. The third copy was bought by Wesson from an Ohio library and was sold to Everett D. Graff. This copy is now held by the Newberry Library in Chicago. No other original copies are believed to exist. In 1960 a microcard printing was made by the Lost Cause Press, Louisville, Kentucky. Several libraries hold this "two card" edition which can be read with suitable magnifying equipment. This Ye Galleon edition is an enlarged facsimile of the Newberry Library copy, to which institution my thanks are extended.

The Leonard history is 122 in Wagner-Camp and L-129 in Howes U.S.-IANA 1650-1950.

Four-hundred-twenty copies of this book were printed in facsimile in the workshop of Glen Adams.

This is Copy Number _165_ .

I

HISTORY

of the

OREGON TERRITORY

FROM ITS FIRST DISCOVERY

UP TO

THE PRESENT TIME

H. L. W. LEONARD, Esq.

YE GALLEON PRESS

FAIRFIELD, WASHINGTON

1980

Library of Congress Cataloging in Publication Data

Leonard, Herman Leroy Williams, 1814?-1872.
    History of the Oregon Territory from its first
discovery up to the present time.

    Reprint of the 1846 ed. printed at Younglove's Steam
Press, Cleveland.
    1. Oregon--History--To 1859. 2. Oregon--Descrip-
tion and travel. I. Title.
F880.L59 1980   979.5   80-10118
ISBN 0-87770-230-6

Biographical Detail

Herman Leroy Williams Leonard was born in Cherry Valley, Otsego County, New York but while yet a boy the family moved to Genesee County. Due to an unusual accident of standing too long in cold water young Leonard developed a stiffening of a knee joint, which made him lame for life. Possibly because he was seriously crippled he became interested in health care and decided to become a physician. He took the complete course of study available at Buffalo Medical College and on his graduation married Miss Eliva E. Conger and started medical practice in Pendleton, Niagara County, to which township his parents had recently moved.

There was through the nineteenth century a general drift of population westward and Dr. Leonard himself moved west to Ohio, first to Albion and then to Strongsville, where he was to remain the rest of his life. Possibly a reason for his remaining so many years in this location was his appointment as postmaster of that town. He was a staunch Democrat in politics and took some part in local political affairs. We note that he was nominated for recorder for the Democratic Convention of 1846. During the Civil War when many Democrats had southern sympathies Dr. Leonard was a Union man.

Dr. Leonard is listed in the 1850 United States census as H.W. Leonard, physician, age 36, born in New York but a resident of Strongsville, Cuyahoga County, Ohio. His wife is listed a "Ellen (?)" age 35, born in New York state. Two sons are also listed, Charles C., age 5 and Clarence age 2. In the 1860 census we find H.L.W. Leonard, physician, age 46, and Charles age 15. Mrs. Leonard died August 29, 1856 at the age of 41. She had been preceded in death by an infant daughter and was survived by two sons, Charles, who would have been eleven at the time of her death, and Lewis aged 'a few months.' As the census record of 1860 does not list Clarence we assume he was not living at this date or at least was not a member of Dr. Leonard's household. Dr. Leonard did not marry again but in later years seems to have had a house keeper as the census of 1870 lists Herman Leonard, physician, age 56, and Orvilla Graves, age 42,

IV

whose occupation was given as 'keeping house.' Also at this address were Charles Graves, age 10, born in Wisconsin; and Otto Graves, age 8, born in Ohio, with occupation of both given as 'at school.' Dr. Leonard died December 4, 1872, aged 58 years, to be followed by his son, Charles, who died March 12, 1874, age 29. Dr. Leonard was highly respected in the community. He apparently began his medical practice in Strongsville about 1841 at age 27 so he was a physician in Strongsville for 31 years, but had also practiced briefly in Pendleton, New York; and Albion, Ohio.

Dr. Leonard wrote his history of the Oregon Territory just before the boundary settlement with Great Britain in 1846, a period when pro-U.S. feeling was running at flood tide. James K. Polk became U.S. President on a platform of "54-40 or fight" and 1846 was the year when a war was manuevered between the United States and Mexico. The political leaders of our country had no difficulty in seeing the possible disastrous consequences should this young a country attempt to fight both Mexico and Britain at once. They were therefore rather anxious to conclude a negotiated settlement with England to divide the Oregon Territory by continuing the boundary westward to the Pacific on the 49th parallel. The warmth of feeling over the Oregon question resulted in the writing of a number of books, both in United States and Britain. Dr. Leonard's history was one of the milder of those books.

Serious students of western United States history will pick up some statements that were more or less acceptable in 1846 but which are not acceptable today. Dr. Leonard, an avid reader, wrote his book without ever having been to the Pacific Northwest. He writes an intelligent summary of early exploration of the west coast of North America but some of this dates are a bit off. More serious is the inclusion of the Maldonado voyage of 1589 which today is considered apocryphal.

The Leonard history of the Oregon Territory was first printed at Younglove's Steam Press, located at Cleveland, Ohio, 1846. It is today an extremely rare book with only three copies known. I do not know of any other printings than the 1846 original and this 1980 Ye Galleon edition. Mr. Moses C. Younglove came to Cleveland about 1836 from Cambridge, Washington County, New York. After trying out several occupations he bought an interest in a book store and a few months later established a job printing and publishing business. In 1845 or 1846 he set up the first steam driven printing press in Cleveland. This was probably the second power press west of the Alleghenies. Other printers of that day used equipment operated by human muscles, generally side lever platens. Mr. Younglove was listed in the 1848 city directory for Cleveland as a bookseller and stationer, and in 1850 and 1860 he was also listed as part of the firm of Younglove and Hoyt, owners of the Cleveland Paper Mill. By 1879 this company had a stock of 300,000 dollars and operated five plants in Ohio, two in Cleveland and one each in Massillon, Canton, and Monroe Falls. Younglove was also a city councilman and a trustee of the Society for Savings bank. The Younglove printing firm was sold in 1853 to Cobb Brothers, which later became Cobb, Andrew & Company. A man of many interests, Moses C. Younglove was founder of the Younglove and Massie Agricultural works and for many years he was president of Kelley Island Lime and Transport Company and of the Lakeside & Marblehead Railroad Company. Mr. Younglove died in Los Angeles on April 13, 1892 and is buried in the Lake View Cemetery near Cleveland.

Glen Adams,
Fairfield, WA.

Sources:

L.G. Stone and T.E. Haynes, *History of Strongsville, Cuyahoa County, Ohio*, 1903, Berea Ohio.
Annals of the Early Settlers' Association of Cuyahoa County, Vol III, no. I-VI, 1892.

VI

REMARKS.

PERHAPS there never was a country or nation, so signally characterized for great and daring enterprise, as the United States; and since their Independence was achieved, they have been making rapid strides towards importance, till their trans-atlantic neighbors are half inclined to look upon them in their true light. One wave of emigration after another has rolled into the vast regions of the West ; settlements have continued to stretch towards the " going down of the sun ; " pioneers have penetrated, in defiance of difficulties and dangers, to the heart of savage countries : laying open the hidden secrets of the wilderness ; leading the way to remote regions of beauty and fertility that might have remained unexplored for ages, and beckoning the sons of " pilgrim fathers," with civilization and agriculture, to follow. Of late, the Territory west of the Rocky Mountains, has been looked upon with much interest, and American citizens have been anxious to gather all the information relative to that country, within their reach. This spirit of inquiry is praiseworthy, and should be encouraged in any people ; and in view of such encouragement, we have been induced to condense a " History of Oregon," *for the people*, that they may know *where it is, whose it is*, and *what it is*. In doing this, the task has by no means been diminutive, — the fragments here thrown together, have been found scattered over a wide field ; and besides Cook's Voyages—Vancouver's Journal—Greenhow's Memoir—Documents accompanying President Adams' Annual Message, 1827—Reports of Congressional Committees on Military Affairs —Anecdotes of an Enterprise Beyond the Rocky Mountains, by Washington Irving, and Adventures of Captain Bonneville, by the same gentleman, we have had recourse to a Report of the Exploring Expedition to Oregon and North California in 1843–4, by Captain J. C. Fremont, of the Topographical Engineers, and Captain Wilkes' Survey of the Mouth of the Columbia, as well as to various other sources, equally authentic. We also have had personal acquaintance with those who have visited this delightful territory, and their report is very similar to that of Caleb and Joshua, after their return from Canaan.   And it augurs well, to see American' citizens, with stout hearts and strong hands, ready to go up and "possess the goodly land."   What Oregon will yet be, in point of wealth and commerce, time must develop; but when we look at its resources, its susceptibilities, we dare hazard the opinion, that before the expiration of the present century, its trade with foreign countries will be equal to that now enjoyed by the States on the Atlantic.   Here is to be a large theatre for the operations of christians and philanthropists. Every day, the lover of his country—of good order, and good society, can see additions made to his large field of labor; and as citizens of a free Republic, may we ever be found ready to defend, and perpetuate our glorious institutions; and though we " WAX FAT," may we never be disposed to "kick," without provocation.   Ever since the last war between the United States and Great Britain, the northern boundary of this Territory has been in an unsettled state, between the two countries. By mutual consent, it was occupied by the citizens of both.   Had circumstances unfortunately occurred, to disturb the harmony of the two nations, this ill-adjusted question would have started up into one of belligerent import, and Oregon, would have become the watchword in the contest for dominion on the shores of the Pacific; but within a few months past, this has been settled on the 49° of N. latitude, by convention, and American jurisdiction extended to the Pacific coast. This will most assuredly have a tendency to induce an increased emigration beyond the mountains —military and trading posts will soon be established along the whole route; and that inauspicious events should ever transpire, at home or abroad, to blast our expectations, may Heaven in mercy forefend.

CLEVELAND, October, 1846.

VIII

HISTORY OF OREGON.

CHAPTER I.

Brief Account of Discoveries made on the North-West Coast of America, by early Navigators.

OREGON, is the name by which that portion of the territory of the United States lying west of the Rocky mountains, is commonly known. It has formed a distinct geographical region for a number of years, but has had no independent official existence till quite recently. The eastern boundary of this territory has always been clearly defined by the Rocky mountains, and its western limit by the Pacific ocean ; and by the treaty between the United States and Spain, known as the Florida Treaty, signed at the city of Washington in 1819, the southern boundary was agreed upon as follows : "A line from the source of the river Arkansas, north or south, as the case might be, to the 42d parallel of latitude, and thence along that parallel, westward, to the Pacific, should form the southern boundary of the United States possessions on the western side of the continent." A few years after the signing of the Florida Treaty, Mexico, which was bounded on the north by this 42d parallel of latitude, became independent of Spain, and in 1828, a treaty was concluded between the United States and this Republic, by which the same line of demarkation agreed on with Spain in 1819, was confirmed by Mexico. There has been much diplomatic contention between the United States and Great Britain, concerning the northern boundary, the United States claiming the parallel of 54° north, or 54° 40', as the rightful limit, while Great Britain has strenuously denied the justice of this claim, on our part, north of Mexico. The United States based their claim to Oregon on the ground of treaty stipulations, priority of discovery, examination and occupation; but to avoid a collision with the British government, and from other reasons, a convention was made between the parties in 1818, and renewed in 1827, by which it was agreed that all of the territory west of the Rocky mountains should be open, for a certain number of years, to both. On the 15th of June, 1846, a convention was concluded at Washington, between the United States and her Majesty the Queen of the United Kingdom of Great Britain and Ireland, who, "deeming it desirable for the future welfare of both countries, that the state of doubt and uncertainty which had heretofore prevailed respecting tho sovereignty and government of the territory on the North-West Coast of America, lying Westward of the Rocky, or Stoney mountains, should be finally terminated by an amicable compromise of the rights mutually asserted by the two parties over said territory, agreed upon and concluded the following :—From the point on the 49th parallel of North latitude, where the boundary laid down in existing treaties and conventions between Great Britain and the United States terminates, the line of boundary between the territories of her Britannic Majesty and those of the United States shall be continued Westward along the 49th parallel of North latitude to the middle of the channel which separates the continent from Vancouver's Island, and thence South. erly through the middle of said channel, and of Fuca Straits, to the Pacific ocean ; provided, however, that the navigation of said channel and straits, South of the 49th parallel of North latitude, remain free and open to both parties," &c. Thus, the northern boundary has finally been fixed on the 49th parallel of N. latitude, to the no little chagrin of certain patriotic politicians, known as *fifty-four-forties*, and here it will remain till by purchase, conquest, or further "compromise of rights," it shall be transferred to a higher northern latitude.

Soon after the settlement of Mexico, in the early part of the sixteenth century, the Spaniards fitted out several expeditions to explore the north-west coast of America, under the superintendence of the celebrated Cortes. In 1534, his lieutenant, Hernando de Grijalva, discovered California, and Cortes himself explored the Gulf which bears the same name. Juan de Cabrillo, who died on the island of San Bernardo in 1543, had examined the coast of California very minutely previous to this time, and sailed as far as 37° 10′ N., and after his death, his pilot, a Greek, continued his discoveries along the coast as far as Cape Blanco, which is in lat. 43° N., and consequently within the present limits of Oregon. About 1582, one Francisco Gali made a voyage from the East Indies to Acapulco, on the west coast of Mexico, and sailed along the coast as high up as the 57th or 58th degree of N. latitude, and gave a very good general and descriptive account of it. Ten years later, and one hundred years after the discovery of America by Columbus, Juan de Fuca discovered and entered the strait which still bears his name. This strait enters the main land in latitude 49° N., and extends about a hundred miles in a S. E. direction, thence changes its course to the N. N. W., and enters the ocean again in latitude 51° N. This adventurer remained nearly a month within the strait, driving his discoveries into the adjacent country, and bartering with the natives; and before leaving took formal possession of the whole country in the name of the King of Spain. In December, 1577, five vessels, fitted out by the English, and placed under the command of Sir Francis Drake, sailed from Plymouth to the west coast of America; not so much for the purpose of making discoveries, as for committing depredations in the Spanish colonies, and making a *loyal piratical cruise*. Sir Francis carried out his intentions to the letter, by robbing and destroying Spanish towns and shipping, wherever he could find them. In 1579 he concluded to return to England by the way of the Cape of Good Hope, and accordingly on the 16th of April of this year he left the west coast of Mexico, sailing as far north as latitude 42°, where contrary winds prevented his further progress. Being thus prevented from continuing his voyage northward, he anchored near the coast; but finding that he could not ride here in safety, he abandoned the ground, and sailed to the south again until he found a safe and commodious harbor in latitude about 38° north, which he run into, to repair his vessels, and continued there from June 17 to July 23. On taking his departure from the continent, he annexed this new country to the British possessions in the name of his sovereign, Queen Elizabeth, and called it New Albion. The spot where Sir Francis anchored to repair was probably St. Francisco's Bay, and the probability is, he did not see the coast north of the 42d degree of latitude, to which point it had been explored by Cabrillo and his pilot, thirty-six years before. In 1588, Maldonado, a Spanish navigator, made a voyage as far north as what is now called Bhering's Straits. In the spring of 1596, the Count de Monterey, Viceroy of Mexico, fitted out three vessels, which left Acapulco, under the command of Sebastian Vizcaino, a nobleman, for the purpose of discovering the north-west passage between the Atlantic and Pacific oceans, which has been searched for diligently, but in vain, by so many navigators since his days. Symptoms of mutiny being discovered among the sailors, this expedition was not carried beyond the limits of

California, and the vessels returned to Mexico the same year. A few years after, Vizcaino made another attempt to survey the coast to the north from Acapulco, and proceeded as far as Cape Blanco, a white promontory, which he discovered and named, in 1603. From this place he was compelled to return, on account of the sickly condition of his men. A small vessel belonging to his expedition proceeded north and discovered the mouth of the river Umpqua, which is within the present limits of Oregon. Vizcaino importuned Monterey to establish colonies along the coast which he had surveyed, for the purpose of facilitating commercial relations with India, as well as to retain possession of the country. But his request being unheeded, he returned to Spain, to solicit the favor of Philip III., and finally succeeded in obtaining royal orders for the execution of his projects ; but he died before his undertaking was consummated, and the government of Spain abandoned all further attempts to colonize the north-west coast of America, or extend their discoveries in that direction, for nearly two centuries afterward. In 1711, Peter the Great, Emperor of Russia, became desirous of extending the area of his dominions, and formed plans for discovering what countries lay beyond the Pacific, which formed the boundary of his empire on the east. He died before his projects were carried into execution ; but Catharine, true to the wishes of her deceased husband, determined to prosecute his plans of discovery with effect, and accordingly in 1728 a small vessel was equipped and sent out by her order, under the command of Vitus Bhering. He steered along the eastern shores of Asia, and before he was aware of it, he passed through the straits, which still bear his name. Bhering visited the American coast again in 1741, and discovered and named Mount St. Elias, and anchored in Admiralty Bay. He was driven ashore soon after on an island, situated in latitude 55° N., which is since known as Bhering's Island, where he died in December, 1741, and thirty of his crew perished on this inhospitable island before spring. The remainder of his men constructed a rude vessel here, in which they put to sea, and returned to Kamschatka with the melancholy tidings. About 1774, the Spaniards, Russians and English renewed their endeavors to find the long looked-for " north-west passage," and to make further explorations of the west coast of America. In this year the Viceroy of Mexico fitted out a corvette, and appointed Juan Perez commander, and Estevan Jose Martinez, pilot. The result of this expedition was kept secret by the government of Spain, until 1802, when the King ordered a brief account of it to be published at Madrid. The instructions given to Perez were, to proceed as far as the 60th degree of north latitude before winter should set in, and then survey the coast carefully, southwardly to Monterey. The first land discovered by him was the N. W. part of Queen Charlotte's Island, in latitude 54° north; he thence proceeded south, and on the 10th of August, 1774, discovered and entered a bay which he named Port St. Lorenzo. In 1778, Captain Cook entered this same bay and called it King George's Sound, having no knowledge of the discoveries made by Perez. This is now called *Nootka Sound*. Perez also sailed into the Straits of Fuca, and named the cape on the south side of the entrance in honor of his pilot, Point Martinez. The next year, or in 1775, another expedition was despatched from San Blas, in Mexico, which proceeded as far north as the 58th degree of latitude, and resulted in very materially adding to the geographical knowledge of the north-west coast. On the 10th of June in this year, the commander of this expedition anchored in a small haven north of Cape Mendocino, and named it Port Trinidad. Before leaving, he erected a cross on shore, bearing an inscription setting forth the time of his visit, and proclaiming to future visitors, the right of Spain to the adjacent country by virtue of this discovery. Captain Vancouver saw this cross standing when he visited the spot in 1793. This expedition also sailed along side of Vancouver's Island, and about the middle of August discovered a promontory which was named Cape St. Roque, and a little distance south of it, in latitude 46° 16', an opening into the land was seen, *which appeared to be the mouth of a river.* This is now known to be the mouth of the Columbia river, which was thus seen, for the first time, by civilized men. In latitude 57° N. they discovered a lofty, conical shaped mountain, on a peninsula, which was named Mount San Jacinto; the point on which it was situated, they called Cape Engano, (Deception.) These, and other localities which were surveyed by the Spaniards at this time, are readily identified at the present time, though now known by different names. Mount San Jacinto is now called Mount Edgecombe, and Port Remedias, and Port Gaudaloupe, which were discovered at the same time, are now known as the Bay of Islands and Norfolk Sound. Here, too, the Spaniards took possession of the country in the name of their Sovereign, on the 19th of August, 1775, as they had done in latitude 46° 16' before.

On the 12th of July, 1776, the British government, still determined to find the "north-west passage," fitted out two ships, the *Resolution* and *Discovery*, and placed them under the command of Captain Cook for this purpose. Cook sailed from Plymouth, with instructions to proceed " to the coast of *New Albion*, endeavoring to fall in with it in latitude 45° N. ; thence to sail northward to the latitude of 65°, or farther, if not obstructed by land or ice." At this parallel he was to commence his examination of the coast, in search of " a water passage, pointing towards Hudson's or Baffin's Bay." If so fortunate as to find such an opening, he was farther instructed, to "endeavor to make his way through it ; but if convinced that the object of his search did not exist, he was to explore the seas north of the 65th parallel, as thoroughly as possible, and give no offence to any of the subjects of any of the governments of Europe, which he might find in that part of the world." March 7th, 1778, Captain Cook arrived off the north-west coast, about a hundred miles north of Cape Mendocino, and commenced his survey of the shore of the continent. On the 23d of the same month, he discovered a point of land projecting into the Pacific, which he called Cape Flattery. He also saw Cape Blanco, which the Spaniards had discovered one hundred and seventy-five years before, to which he now gave the name of Cape Gregory. Cook *passed the mouth of the Columbia river and the Strait of Fuca without discovering them,* although he made diligent search for the latter, *south* of Cape Flattery. He sailed northward as far as Bhering's Strait, and his researches have proved of great importance, as the relative location of many points along this coast were but inaccurately known, and others had never been seen. He remained within Port St. Lorenzo several weeks trading with the natives, and claimed the honor of being its first discoverer, and called it King George's Sound, as we have before stated, though the Indians gave satisfactory indications of having had intercourse with civilization before. They were not struck with that surprise at the appearance of his ships, which the South Sea Islanders and other savages manifested at the first sight ; at the report of his guns, which were discharged in their presence, they did not appear startled ; and they had many articles in their possession which were evidently of Spanish manufacture. The English government have attached great importance to the discoveries made by Captain Cook at this time, and by virtue of them, have laid claim to a great part of the territory of Oregon. Americans see about as much justice in this claim, as in many others, which that government has advanced against other parts of Christendom.

The French never attempted to explore the north-west coast till 1785. In this year La Perouse left France on a voyage of discovery, and was instructed to survey those parts of the N. W. coast of America which had not been examined by Captain Cook, and which the Russian navigators had not mentioned. La Perouse was not able, as we are informed, to devote much time to this examination, but sailed along the coast from Mount St. Elias, as far as Monterey. The discoveries he made were of no importance.

In 1791, Captain Marchand, in a French merchant ship, sailed along this coast as far as the entrance of Clyoquot Bay, near Nootka Sound. He landed on one of the islands belonging to King George the Third's Archipelago, in the vicinity of Mount Edgecombe, and remained there two weeks trading with the natives. His journal discloses no important discoveries, in regard to the coast he visited.

This same year the British government sent out another expedition, under the command of Captain Vancouver, to prosecute the projects which had been frustrated by the death of Captain Cook. Vancouver took command of the *Discovery*, himself, while the *Chatham* accompanied him under the command of Lieutenant Broughton, and on the 10th of April, 1792, arrived on the north-west coast, near Cape Mendocino. He proceeded northward from thence, and near the 43d parallel N. he *discovered* a promontory which corresponded in location with *Cape Blanco*, of the Spaniards, and *Cape Gregory*, of Captain Cook, but he thought proper to give it the name of *Cape Oxford*. From this point he continued coasting to the north, and *passed the mouth of the Columbia river, in lat. 46° 19', without calling to examine it.* The following extract from his journal will be satisfactory on this point : " On the 27th of April, noon brought us up with a very conspicuous point of land, composed of a cluster of hummocks, moderately high, and projecting into the sea. On the south side of this promontory was the appearance of an inlet, or small river, the land not indicating it to be of any great extent, nor did it seem accessible for vessels of our burthen. This promontory I was at first induced to believe was Cape Shoalwater, but on examining its latitude, I presumed it to be Cape Disappointment, and the opening south of it, Deception Bay. This cape was found to be in latitude 46° 19' N., and longitude 136°

6′ W. *Not considering this opening worthy of more attention,* I continued our pursuit to the north-west," &c. Two days after entering the above extract on his journal, Vancouver met Captain Gray, of Boston, in the American ship Columbia, and had an interview with him. This was at the entrance of the Strait of Fuca, and Vancouver enters in his journal under date of 29th of April, 1792, that Captain Gray informed him " of his having entered an inlet to the northward, in latitude 54½ degrees, in which he sailed to latitude 56° without discovering its termination, and of his having been at the mouth of a river in latitude 46° 10′, where the reflux was so strong as to prevent his entering for nine days." On the 30th of April, he farther says : " We have now explored a part of the American continent, extending nearly 215 leagues, under the most fortunate and favorable circumstances of wind and weather. So minutely has this extensive coast been inspected, that *the surf has been constantly seen to break on its shores, from the mast-head,* and it was but in a few intervals when the distance precluded its being visible from the deck. It must be considered as a very singular circumstance, that in so great an extent of sea coast, *we should not have seen the appearance of any opening in its shores,* which presented any certain prospect of affording shelter : *the whole coast forming one compact, solid, nearly straight barrier against the sea. I was thoroughly convinced, that we could not possibly have passed any safe navigable opening, harbor, or place of security for shipping on this coast, from Cape Mendocino to the promontory of Classet,*" or Cape Flattery. Captain Vancouver visited the Columbia river after this, and his lieutenant, Broughton, explored it by the aid of Captain Gray's chart ; ascending it upwards of a hundred miles, until within view of a mountain covered with snow, to which he gave the name of Mount Hood, which it still retains. As we before remarked, Great Britain claimed the territory of Oregon, by virtue of discoveries made by Captain Cook ; she also claims it on the ground of the *discovery* of the Columbia river by Captain Vancouver ; she also lays claim to it, on the ground of the discovery of the Columbia, by one John Meares, a lieutenant in the British navy.

We will now look at the merit which the English have awarded to Lieut. Meares, in the *discovery* of the Columbia river. Two vessels, the *Felice* and the *Iphigenia,* sailed from Macao in January, 1788, for the north-west coast of America, to engage in the fur trade, under the direction of Meares, who was then on a half-pay. Meares sailed in the Felice, and the Iphigenia carried a British supercargo, named Douglas. These two vessels, however, were furnished with *Portuguese officers*, both had *Portuguese passports*, and papers showing them to be the property of a *Portuguese merchant* at Macao, *Juan Cavallo ;* they had instructions in the *Portuguese language*, and sailed under *Portuguese colors. Who ever heard of an English exploring expedition under similar circumstances ?* In the volume of their instructions was a passage which read as follows : " Should you meet with any Russian, English, or Spanish vessels, you will treat them with civility, and allow them, if they are authorized, to examine your papers ; should they however, attempt to seize you, or carry you out of your way, you will prevent it by every means in your power, and repel force by force." Now, if this was purely an English expedition, why instruct them to treat *English* vessels, which they might meet, with civility ? Why afraid of being seized, or carried out of the way, by their own countrymen ? Why were Portuguese officers, Portuguese passports and Portuguese flags necessary ?

We can prove the United States' title to every inch of Oregon, *even up to 54° 40'*, more readily than we can answer either of these interrogatories. This expedition seems to be nothing but a private undertaking of Juan Cavallo, a Portuguese merchant of Macao. Meares published an account of his voyage, in England, in 1790, in which we are informed that he discovered a headland, in latitude 46° 47', which he called Cape Shoalwater ; and that " sailing along the coast, a high bluff promontory bore " off us south-east, at the distance of only four leagues. We " pleased ourselves with the expectation of its being Cape St. " Roque, of the Spaniards, near which they are said to have " found a good port. After we had rounded the promontory a " large bay opened to our view, that bore a very promising ap- " pearance, and into which we steered with every encouraging " expectation. The high land that formed the boundaries of the " bay, was at a great distance, and a flat, level country occupied " the intervening space. As we steered in, the water shoaled to " nine, eight, and seven fathoms, when breakers were seen from " the deck right ahead, and from the mast-head they were ob- " served to extend across the bay ; we therefore hauled out, and " directed our course to the opposite shore, to see if there was " any channel, or if we could discover any port. The name of " *Cape Disappointment* was given to the promontory, and the

" bay obtained the title of *Deception Bay.* By an indifferent
" meridian observation, it lies in latitude 46° 10′ north. *We can
" now safely assert, that there is no such river as that of St.
" Roque,* laid down in *the Spanish charts*," &c. &c.

Here, then, we can see the strength of Britain's claim to Oregon, based on Meares' discovery of the Columbia river, when
Meares himself positively denies there being any such river, and
he calls the mouth of the river, into which he entered unawares,
nothing but a bay. Notwithstanding this assertion of Meares,
the Brtish Plenipotentiaries in 1826 solemnly declared to the
United States Minister, that " Great Britain can show, that in
" 1788, that is, four years before Gray entered the mouth of the
" Columbia river, Mr. Meares, a lieutenant of the royal navy,
" who had been *sent by the East India Company,* on a trading
" expedition to the North-West Coast of America, had already
" minutely explored that coast, from the 49th to the 45th degree
" of north latitude—had taken formal possession of the Strait of
" Fuca in the name of his sovereign—had purchased land,
" trafficked and formed treaties with the natives, and had actually
" entered the bay of Columbia, to the northern headland of which,
" he gave the name of Cape Disappointment; a name
" which it bears to this day." Though they further add—" It
" must indeed be admitted that Mr. Gray, finding himself in the
" bay formed by the discharge of the waters of the Columbia into
" the Pacific, was the first to ascertain that this bay formed the
" outlet of a great river, a discovery which had escaped Lieuten-
" ant Meares, when in 1788, he entered the same bay."

These are substantially the grounds of the British government,
on which its *ownership* of Oregon has rested, and by virtue of
which it has denied that the United States ever possessed a foot of
earth north of the 42d parallel of latitude on the north-west coast
of America. We have mentioned the most important expeditions sent out to this coast by the different European governments
from the first discovery of the continent to 1792, and shall proceed with American discoveries, and substantiate the claim of the
United States to the " whole of Oregon," which we consider
" clear and unquestionable."

CHAPTER II.

Americans turn their attention to the North Western Fur Trade at the close of the War of the Revolution. Voyage of Capts. Gray and Kendrick, and their discoveries· Fatal tragedy, and loss of the ship Tonquin, at Vancouver's Island.

That spirit of enterprise which has ever characterized the citizens of our Republic, induced several American merchants, soon after the close of the struggle for Independence, to make arrangements for carrying on an extensive, and, as they hoped, lucrative fur trade, on the coast of the north Pacific ocean.— Until the close of the late war with Great Britain, there was no direct trade carried on between the north-west coast and China, by other than American vessels, and under the "stars and stripes" of the United States. As early as 1791, seven vessels from the United States, and the most if not all of them, from New England, arrived on the north-west coast ; and in the prosecution of this business, many discoveries have been made, many dangers encountered, many hardships overcome, and some vessels and many lives have been lost. On the 30th of September, 1787, Captains Gray and Kendrick, of Boston, sailed in the ships *Columbia* and *Washington*, for the north-west coast, and in September, 1788, arrived at Nootka Sound, where they spent the following winter. The next year Captain Gray returned to the United States by way of China, while Captain Kendrick remained on the coast. Before leaving for Canton, Gray sailed up the Strait of Fuca 50 miles, and from information gathered from the natives, was satisfied that this strait communicated with the Pacific, at a place which he had the year previous given the name of Pinckard's Sound. In 1791, Captain Gray made a second voyage, and on the 7th of May, 1792, discovered a safe harbor in latitude 47° N., which, in honor of one of the owners of the ship Columbia, he called Bulfinch's Harbor. According to Gray's own account, he discovered the mouth of the Columbia, on the 11th of May, 1792, and ascended that river twenty miles, examining the country and trading with the natives, and remained in the river till the 20th of the same month. He describes it as being a broad and rapid stream, and the water peculiarly fresh and pure. He named the river after his gallant ship, and the promontory north of its mouth he called Cape Hancock, and that on the south, Cape

Adams. In the winter of 1791-2, he built and launched a schooner at *Clyoquot*, near Nootka, and called it the *Enterprise*. This was the first vessel ever built by citizens of the United States on the north-west coast, *or in Oregon*. In August, 1791, while lying in Nootka Sound, Captain Kendrick became suspicious that if he put out to sea, the Spaniards, who were hovering about him, would seize his vessel. He accordingly resolved to force his way, if possible, through a passage which he was confident opened to the north-westward into the Pacific. He was successful in his undertaking, and the outlet which he thus discovered he named Massachusetts Sound. About this time Kendrick purchased of *Maquinna* and other native Chiefs, large tracts of land near Nootka Sound, which purchase is described as " a tract of delightful country, comprehending four degrees of latitude, or *two hundred and forty miles square*." The deeds for this land were registered in the office of the American Consul in China. It was with considerable difficulty that Captain Gray entered the mouth of the Columbia, on account of sand bars and breakers.— A boat was well manned and sent on shore to a village on the beach, but all the inhabitants fled with consternation, excepting the aged and infirm. The kind manner in which these were treated and the presents given to them, gradually lured back the others, and a friendly intercourse took place. They had never seen a ship or a white man before. When they had first descried the *Columbia,* they had supposed it a floating island ; then some monster of the deep ; but when they saw the boat putting for shore, with human beings on board, they considered them sent by the *Great Spirit*, to ravage the country and devour the inhabitants. Now if the principle is correct, that "*the discovery and occupation of the mouth of a river, gives the title to the entire territory drained by it*," should not our northern limits be carried to about 54°, or 54° 40'? We submit the question to disinterested *forty-niners*. Or, *if according to the usages of nations, any nation taking possession of unoccupied territory, acquires the right to form settlements and grant lands over one half the space between the point thus actually in possession, and any point occupied by the settlements of any nation,* where would the northern boundary of Oregon be located? The most southern point of country taken possession of by Captain Cook, was at the mouth of Cook's River, in latitude 61° 30' N. Astoria, or Fort Clatsop, at the mouth of the Columbia, taken possession of by Lewis and Clarke, and afterwards occupied by the Pacific Fur Company, is in latitude 46° 18'. The mean distance between these two places would be our northern limit, and this would bring it at 53° 54' N. Let us take a *precedent*, established by Great Britain. After England had made discoveries and planted colonies on the Atlantic coast, she claimed, and granted to her subjects, the lands from the Atlantic entirely across the continent, to the Pacific.— For examples, illustrating this, see the Colonial Charters of Virginia, Massachusetts Bay, and Connecticut. Even now, by virtue of the discovery and occupation of Hudson's Bay, England claims by this *rule of contiguity*, an extension of jurisdiction westward to the Rocky Mountains. If we apply this rule in squaring our rights, our claim to the territory of Oregon is easily established—*the lion is bearded in his own den.* We shall hereafter give a short account of the stipulations of the treaties of Utrecht, Versailles, and Ghent, and also the Convention of St. Petersburg, in confirmation of the United States' claim. In 1763, shortly after the Canadas had fallen into the possession of the British, Captain Jonathan Carver, of Massachusetts, first projected an expedition across the continent, between the 43d and 46th parallels of north latitude, to the shores of the Pacific ocean.— His object was to ascertain the breadth of the continent at its broadest part, and to fix on some place on the Pacific coast where government might establish a post to facilitate the discovery of the "north-west passage" to the Hudson's Bay. Carver did not get ready to start on his journey till the summer of 1766, when he left Boston, and passed the two following years west of the Great Lakes, and in the vicinity of the head waters of the Mississippi. This enterprising traveller never proceeded farther west, being twice baffled in his endeavors to accomplish this great undertaking. He was the first to learn from the natives, that a great river, called the *Oregon*, run westward from the Mountains to the Pacific. It is in his journal that the word *Oregon* is first found, and its etymology and meaning has never been determined. It was Carver's opinion that this great river emptied itself into the Pacific, somewhere about the Straits of Annian, and at its mouth would be the most favorable location for a settlement, to open a more direct communication with China and the English settlements in the East Indies. On the 18th of January, 1803, President Jefferson sent a confidential Message to the Congress of the United States, in which he recommended that measures should be adopted for the exploration of the country west of the Rocky Mountains, without delay. Congress approved the President's recommendation, and Merriweather Lewis and William Clark were commissioned to carry into operation the enterprise projected by Carver. Messrs. Lewis and Clark were instructed by the President to look for some stream running westward from the mountains, "whether the Columbia, the Oregon, the Colorado, or any other which might offer the most direct and practicable water communication across the continent, for the purposes of commerce ;" and to trace the same to its termination in the Pacific. In October, 1804, they had only reached the country of the Mandan Indians, sixteen hundred miles above the mouth of the Missouri, and here they remained till April, 1805. They explored the Missouri to its source among the Rocky Mountains ; passed through the stupendous gates of the dividing ridge, hitherto unknown to white men, and soon discovered a number of streams flowing westward. They embarked in canoes upon one of the streams, on the 7th of October, 1805, and run down to a river which they called *Lewis'*, and soon after they discovered another tributary, which was named *Clark's* ; and on the 15th of November, 1805, they had followed the Columbia to its mouth, where their countryman Gray, had anchored thirteen years before. They had now made a journey of four thousand miles. A landing was made on the north side of the mouth of the Columbia river, but the party soon crossed over to the south, where an encampment was formed, and named *Fort Clatsop*, and here they remained during the winter of 1805-6. They began their return to the United States, March 13th, 1806 ; but before breaking up their encampment, they wrote an account of their journey, on parchment, one copy of which was posted up in the fort, and a number more distributed among the natives, and at the same time possession was taken of the territory, by authority and in the name of the United States. They proceeded to the falls of the Columbia, a distance of one hundred and twenty-five miles from the Pacific, in canoes which had been constructed for the purpose, and then took the land. Upon reaching the Rocky Mountains, the company was divided ; the party commanded by Captain Lewis continuing directly east to the falls of the Missouri, while Clark bore off to the south, so as to come upon the head waters of the Yellow Stone. The parties joined each other again at the confluence of the Yellow Stone and Missouri, and on the 23d of September, 1806, reached St. Louis in safety.

The favorable report made by Messrs. Lewis and Clark, led to the formation of large commercial enterprizes, both in the United

States and British America ; and clearly demonstrated the practicability of establishing a line of communications across the continent, from the Atlantic to the Pacific ocean. It was as though another *El Dorado* or a new *Gold Coast* had been discovered. In 1808, an association was formed at St. Louis, called the *Missouri Fur Company.* Another was formed in New York, by John Jacob Astor, in 1810, and known as the *Pacific Fur Company.* The first permanent post ever established in the territory of Oregon, or in the country drained by the Columbia and its tributaries, was by the Missouri Fur Company, on the head waters of Lewis' river ; but they were obliged to abandon this in 1810, on account of difficulty in getting supplies, and the hostility of the savages with which they were surrounded. The main feature of Mr. Astor's plan was to establish a line of trading posts along the Missouri and the Columbia, to the mouth of the latter, where was to be established the chief trading house or factory. Inferior posts would be founded in the interior, and on all the tributaries of the Columbia, to trade with the Indians ; these posts would draw their supplies from the factory at the mouth of the river, and bring to it the peltries they collected.— Coasting craft would be built and fitted out, also, at the main establishment, to trade, at favorable seasons, all along the north-west coast, and return, with the proceeds of their voyage, to this place of deposite. Thus all the Indian trade, both of the interior and the coast, would converge at this point, and thus derive its sustenance. A ship was to be sent annually from New York to this main establishment with re-inforcements and supplies, and with merchandize suited to the trade. It would take on board the furs collected during the preceding year, carry them to Canton, invest the proceeds in the rich merchandize of China, and return thus freighted to New York. For the effectual prosecution of this plan, Mr. Astor engaged as partners in the Company, Alexander McKay, who had accompanied Sir Alexander McKenzie in both of his expeditions to the north-west coast of America in 1789 and 1793, and Donald McKenzie and Duncan McDougal, who had been in the employ of the British North-West Fur Company. Wilson P. Hunt was subsequently added to the firm, and as he was a native born citizen of the United States, he was selected by Mr. Astor to be his chief agent, and to represent him in the contemplated establishment. Articles of agreement were entered into between Mr. Astor and these gentlemen, in June, 1810, according to which Mr. Astor was to be at the head of the

Company, and to manage its affairs in New York. He was to furnish vessels, goods, arms, ammunition, provisions, and all other necessaries for the enterprise at first cost and charges, provided that they did not, at any time, involve an advance of more than four hundred thousand dollars. The Association, if successful, was to continue twenty years; a general meeting of the Company was to be held annually at Columbia river, for the investigation and regulation of its affairs; and should the enterprise be found unprofitable, the parties had full power to abandon and dissolve it within five years, for which term Mr. Astor agreed to bear all the loss that might be incurred; after which, it was to be borne by all the partners, in proportion to their respective investments. An agent, appointed for the term of five years was to reside at the principal establishment on the north-west coast, and Mr. Hunt was the one chosen for the first term. In carrying out this scheme, two expeditions were devised by Mr. Astor, one by sea, the other over land. The former was to take out the requisites for establishing a fortified trading post at the mouth of the Columbia river, and the latter was to be conducted by Mr. Hunt, up the Missouri and across the Rocky Mountains to the same point. In his route Mr. Hunt was to select places where interior trading posts might be located. As the expedition by sea took its departure a few months before the one by land, it will come first under consideration. The ship *Tonquin*, of two hundred and ninety tons, and mounting ten guns, was provided by Mr. Astor, and manned with a crew of twenty men. The command of the vessel was entrusted to Jonathan Thorn, of New York, a lieutenant in the United States navy, on leave of absence. Lieutenant Thorn was well fitted to take charge of an expedition of this kind, being firm, courageous, and accustomed to naval discipline, having distinguished himself in our war with Tripoli. Several of the partners and clerks were to embark in the ship, which also carried an assortment of merchandize for trading with the natives; the frame of a schooner to be employed in the coasting trade; mechanics for the supply of the colony, and seeds for the cultivation of the soil, and whatever else was deemed necessary for the supply and maintainance of the establishment. On the 8th of September, 1810, the Tonquin put to sea; and to guard against any interruption of the voyage by an armed brig said to be off the harbor, Mr. Astor had applied to Commodore Rodgers, at that time commanding at New York, to give the Tonquin safe convoy off the coast. The Commodore accordingly directed captain Hull, of the frigate Constitution, to afford her the required protection, and the wind being fresh from the south-west, the ship was soon hurried out of sight of land, and free from the apprehended danger. The frigate gave her " God speed!" and left her to her course.

On the 7th of December, they anchored at Port Egmont, on one of the Falkland Islands, and remained four days taking in water and making repairs. December the 25th, they doubled Cape Horn, and on the 11th of February, 1811, arrived at Owhyhee, or Hawaii, one of the Sandwich Islands. Here they remained till the 28th, when they again set sail for the sterner regions of the north-west coast, and on the 22d of March, the Tonquin arrived at the mouth of the Columbia. The aspect of the river and the adjacent coast, was wild and dangerous. The mouth of the Columbia is more than four miles wide, with a peninsula and promontory on one side, and a long low point of land on the other ; between which a sand-bar and chain of breakers nearly block up the entrance. A strong wind from the north-west, sent a rough tumbling sea upon the coast, which broke upon the sand-bar in furious surges, and extended a sheet of foam almost across the mouth of the river. Under these circumstances, Captain Thorn did not think it prudent to approach within three leagues of the mouth, until the bar should be sounded and the channel ascertained. Accordingly, at one o'clock, P. M., Mr. Fox, the chief mate of the Tonquin, accompanied by John Martin, an old seaman, and three Canadians, set off in the whale boat, which is represented as small in size and crazy in condition, to perform this dangerous service. All eyes were strained after the little boat as it pulled for shore, rising and sinking with the huge rolling waves, until a mere speck, it entered among the foaming breakers, and was soon lost to view. Evening set in—night succeeded and passed away, and morning returned, but without the return of the boat. As the wind had moderated, the ship stood near to the land, so as to command a view of the river's mouth. Nothing was to be seen but a wild chaos of tumbling waves breaking upon the bar, and apparently forming a foaming barrier from shore to shore. Towards night the Tonquin stood out to gain sea-room, and gloom was visible in every countenance. Another weary and watchful night succeeded, during which the wind subsided, and the weather became serene. On the following day, the ship having drifted near the land, anchored in fourteen fathoms water to the northward of the promontory, called Cape

Disappointment. The pinnace was then manned, and set off in the hope of learning something of the whale-boat. The surf, however, broke with such violence along the shore that they could find no landing place. Several of the natives appeared on the beach and made signs to them to row round the cape, but they thought it most prudent to return to the ship. The wind now springing up, the Tonquin got under way, and stood in to seek the channel; but was again deterred, by the frightful aspect of the breakers, from venturing within a league. Here she hove to, and Mr. Mumford, the second mate, was despatched with four hands, in the pinnace, to sound across the channel until he should find four fathoms depth. The pinnace entered among the breakers, but was near being lost, and with difficulty got back to the ship. The captain insisted that Mr. Mumford had steered too much to the southward. He now turned to Mr. Aikin, an able seaman who was destined to command the schooner intended for the coasting trade, and ordered him, together with John Coles, sail-maker, Stephen Weekes, armorer, and two Sandwich Islanders, to proceed ahead and take soundings, while the ship should follow under easy sail. In this way they proceeded until Aikin had ascertained the channel, when signal was given from the ship for him to return on board. He was then within pistol shot, but so furious was the current, and tumultuous the breakers, that the boat became unmanageable, and was hurried away, the crew crying out piteously for assistance. In a few moments she could not be seen from the ship's deck. Some of the passengers climbed to the mizzen top, and beheld her struggling to reach the ship; but shortly after she broached broadside to the waves, and her case seemed desperate. The attention of those on board the ship was now called to their own safety. They were in shallow water; the vessel struck repeatedly, the waves broke over her, and there was danger of foundering. At length she got into seven fathoms water, and the wind lulling, and the night coming on, cast anchor. With the darkness their anxieties increased. The wind again whistled, the sea roared, the gloom was only broken by the ghastly glare of the foaming breakers, the minds of the seamen were full of dreary apprehensions, and some of them fancied they heard the cries of their lost comrades mingling with the uproar of the elements. For a time, too, the rapidly ebbing tide threatened to sweep them from their precarious anchorage. At length the reflux of the tide, and the springing up of the wind, enabled them to quit their dangerous situation, and take shelter in a small bay within Cape Disappointment, where they rode in safety during the remainder of a stormy night, and enjoyed a short interval of refreshing sleep. With the light of day returned their cares and anxieties. They looked from the mast-head over a wild coast, and wilder sea, but could discover no trace of the two boats and their crews that were missing. Several of the natives came on board with peltries, but there was no disposition to trade. They were interrogated by signs after the lost boats, but could not understand the inquiries. Parties now went on shore and scoured the neighborhood, one of which was headed by Captain Thorn. They had not proceeded far when they discovered Weekes, the armorer. His story was short and melancholy. He and his companions had found it impossible to manage the boat, having no rudder, and being beset by rapid and whirling currents and boisterous surges. After long struggling they had let her go at the mercy of the waves, tossing about, sometimes with her bow, sometimes with her broadside to the surges, threatened each instant with destruction, yet repeatedly escaping, until a large sea broke over and swamped her. Weekes was overwhelmed by the boiling waves, but emerging above the surface, looked round for his companions. The two Sandwich Islanders were discovered stripping themselves of their clothing that they might swim more freely, but Aikin and Coles were not to be seen. Weekes being joined by the Islanders, they united their forces, and succeeded in turning the boat upon her keel ; then bearing down her stern and rocking her, they forced out so much of the water that she was able to bear the weight of a man without sinking. One of the Islanders now got in, and in a little while bailed out the water with his hands. The other swam about and collected the oars, and they all three got once more on board. By this time the tide had swept them beyond the breakers, and Weekes called on his companions to row for land. They were so chilled and benumbed by the cold, that they lost all heart, and absolutely refused to obey. Weekes was equally chilled, but had superior sagacity and self-command. He counteracted the tendency to stupor which cold produces, by keeping himself in constant exercise ; and seeing that the vessel was advancing, and that every thing depended on himself, he set to work to scull the boat clear of the bar, and into quiet water. Towards midnight one of the poor Islanders expired : his companion threw himself on his corpse, and could not be persuaded to leave him. As the horrors of this dismal night wore

away, and day dawned, Weekes found himself near the land. He
steered for it, and with the help of the surf, ran his boat high
upon a sandy beach. Thus Weekes and this Islander were the
only survivors of the crew of the jolly-boat, and no trace of Fox
and his party was ever discovered.

The loss of eight men on the first approach to the coast, had
a tendency to cast a gloom over the spirits of the whole party,
and was regarded by the superstitious, as an omen that boded ill
luck to the enterprise.

Captain Thorn had been instructed to land his cargo at the
mouth of the Columbia, wherever the site for a trading house
should be selected, and thence continue his voyage northward
along the coast, and return in the fall. Accordingly, on the 12th
of April, the launch was freighted with all things necessary for
the purpose, and sixteen persons departed in her to commence the
establishment, leaving the Tonquin to follow as soon as the harbor could be sounded. Crossing the wide mouth of the river, the
party landed on the south side, and encamped at the bottom of a
small bay within Point George. The situation chosen for the
fortified post was on an elevation facing to the north, with the
wide estuary, its sand-bars and tumultuous breakers spread out
before it, and the promontory of Cape Disappointment, fifteen
miles distant, closing the prospect to the left. The Tonquin shortly
afterwards made her way through the intricate channel, and came
to anchor in the little bay, and was saluted from the encampment
with three volleys of musketry and three cheers. She returned
the salute with three cheers and three guns. The residence,
store-house and powder magazine were soon built of logs and
covered with bark. The timbers intended for the frame of the
coasting vessel, were landed and put together ; and a garden spot
cleared and sowed with seed. It was now thought by the party
that this metropolis *in embryo* should have a name; and it was
accordingly called, in honor of its founder, ASTORIA.

The neighboring Indians now swarmed about the place. Some
brought a few land-otter and sea-otter skins to barter, but in very
scanty parcels ; the greater number came prying about to gratify their curiosity, for they are said to be impertinently inquisi-
tive ; while not a few came with no other design than to pilfer ;
the laws of *meum* and *tuum* being but slightly respected among
them.

On the 5th of June, the Tonquin got under way and stood out
to sea, with a fine breeze and swelling canvas, and swept off

gaily on her trading voyage, from which she never returned. It was unanimously determined that Mr. M'Kay, one of the partners, should go in her as supercargo, taking with him Mr. Lewis as ship's clerk, and the whole number of persons on board amounted to twenty-three. In leaving the mouth of the river, Captain Thorn picked up from a fishing canoe, an Indian named Lamaree, who had already made two voyages along the coast, and knew something of the languages of the various tribes. He agreed to accompany them as interpreter. Steering to the north, they arrived in a few days at Vancouver's Island, and anchored in the harbor of Neweetee, very much against the advice of the Indian interpreter, who warned them against the perfidious character of the natives of this part of the coast. Mr. M'Kay, accompanied by a few men, went on shore to a village to visit Wicananish, the chief of the surrounding territory, six of the natives remaining on board as hostages. In the morning before Mr. M'Kay had returned to the ship, great numbers of the natives came off in their canoes to trade, headed by two sons of the chief. As they brought abundance of sea-otter skins, and there was every appearance of a brisk trade, Captain Thorn did not wait for the return of M'Kay, but spread out his wares upon the deck, making a tempting display of blankets, cloths, knives, beads, fish-hooks, and expecting a prompt and profitable sale. The Indians, however, were not so eager and simple as had been supposed, having learned the art of bartering, and the value of merchandise, from the casual traders along the coast. They were guided, too, by a shrewd old chief named Nookamis, who had grown gray in traffic with New England skippers, and prided himself upon his acuteness, and all the world knows, that an apt scholar can soon learn the science of bargaining when placed under the tuition of such teachers. His opinion seemed to regulate the market. When Captain Thorn made what he considered a liberal offer for an otter skin, the wily old Indian treated it with scorn, and asked more than double. His comrades all took their cue from him, and not an otter skin was to be had at a reasonable rate. The old fellow, however, overshot his mark, and mistook the character of the man he was treating with. Thorn was a plain, straight-forward sailor, who never had two minds nor two prices in his dealings, was somewhat deficient in patience and pliancy, and totally wanting in the trickery of traffic. He had a vast deal of stern, but honest pride in his nature, and, moreover, held the whole race of savages in sovereign contempt. Abandoning all further attempts to trade with his bantering customers, he thrust his hands into his pockets and paced up and down the deck in sullen silence. The cunning old Indian followed the captain to and fro, holding out a sea-otter skin to him at every turn, and pestering him to trade. Finding other means unavailing, he suddenly changed his tone, and began to ridicule the insignificant prices he offered. This was too much for the patience of the captain, who was never remarkable for relishing a joke, especially when at his own expense. Turning suddenly upon his persecutor, he snatched the proffered otter skin from his hands, rubbed it in his face, and forced him over the side of the ship, with a complimentary kick, to hasten his exit. He then knocked the peltries to the right and left about the deck, and broke up the market in the most ignominious manner. Old Nookamis made for the shore in a furious passion, in which he was joined by Shewish, one of the sons of Wicananish, who went off breathing vengeance, and the ship was soon abandoned by the natives.

When Mr. M'Kay returned on board, the interpreter related what had passed, and begged him to prevail on the captain to make sail, as, from his knowledge of the temper and pride of the people of the place, he was sure they would resent the indignity offered to one of their chiefs. Mr. M'Kay, who himself possessed some experience of Indian character, went to the captain, who was still pacing the deck, and represented the danger to which his hasty act had exposed the vessel, and urged him to weigh anchor. The captain made light of his counsels, and pointed to his cannon and fire-arms as a sufficient safeguard against naked savages. Further remonstrances only provoked taunting replies and sharp altercations. The day passed away without any signs of hostility, and at night the captain retired as usual to his cabin, taking no more than usual precaution.

On the following morning, at daybreak, while the captain and M'Kay were yet asleep, a canoe came alongside in which were twenty Indians, commanded by young Shewish. They were unarmed, their aspect and demeanor friendly, and they held up their otter skins, and made signs indicative of a wish to trade. The officers of the watch, perceiving the Indians to be without weapons, and having received no orders to the contrary, readily permitted them to mount the deck. Another canoe soon succeeded, the crew of which was likewise admitted. In a little time, other canoes came off, and Indians were soon clambering into the vessel on all sides. The officers of the watch now felt alarmed, and called to Captain Thorn and Mr. M'Kay. By the time they came upon deck, it was thronged with savages. The interpreter noticed that many of the natives wore short mantles of skins, and intimated to Mr. M'Kay that they were secretly armed. Mr. M'Kay urged the captain to clear the ship, and get under way. He again made light of the advice ; but the augmented swarm of canoes about the ship, and the numbers still putting off from the shore, at length awakened his distrust, and he ordered some of the crew to weigh anchor, while some were sent aloft to make sail. The Indians now offered to trade with the captain on his own terms, prompted, apparently, by the approaching departure of the ship. Accordingly, a hurried trade was commenced. The main articles sought by the savages in barter, were knives ; as fast as some were supplied, they moved off, and others succeeded. By degrees, weapons were thus distributed about the deck. The anchor was now nearly up, the sails were loose, and the captain, in a loud and peremptory tone, ordered the ship to be cleared. In an instant a signal yell was given : it was echoed on every side ; knives and war-clubs were brandished in every direction ; and the savages rushed upon their marked victims. The first that fell was Mr. Lewis, the ship's clerk. He was leaning over a bale of blankets, with folded arms, engaged in bargaining, when he received a deadly stab in the back, and fell down the companion-way. Mr. M'Kay, who was seated on the taffrail, sprang on his feet, but was instantly knocked down with a war-club and flung backwards into the sea, where he was dispatched by the women in the canoes. In the meantime, Captain Thorn made desperate fight against fearful odds. He was a powerful as well as resolute man, but he had come on deck without weapons. Shewish, the young chief, singled him out as his peculiar prey, and rushed upon him at the first outbreak. The captain had barely time to draw a clasp-knife, with one blow of which he laid the young savage dead at his feet. Several of the stoutest of the followers of Shewish now set upon him. He defended himself vigorously, dealing crippling blows to right and left, and strewing the quarter deck with the slain and wounded. His object was to fight his way to the cabin, where there were fire-arms ; but he was hemmed in with foes, covered with wounds, and faint from the loss of blood. For an instant he leaned upon the tiller wheel, when a blow from behind, with a war-club, felled him to the deck, where he was dispatched with knives and thrown overboard.

While this was transacting upon the quarter-deck, a mixed

fight was going on throughout the ship. The crew fought desperately with knives, handspikes, and whatever weapons they could seize upon in the moment of surprise. They were soon, however, overpowered by numbers, and mercilessly butchered.

As to the seven who had been sent aloft to make sail, they contemplated with horror, the carnage that was going on below. Being destitute of weapons, they let themselves down by the running rigging, in hopes of getting between decks. One fell in the attempt, and was instantly dispatched; another received a death-blow in the back as he was descending; a third, Stephen Weekes, the armorer, was mortally wounded as he was getting down the hatchway. The remaining four made good their retreat into the cabin, where they found Mr. Lewis, the clerk, still alive, though mortally wounded. Barricading the cabin door, they broke holes through the companion way, and with the muskets and ammunition which were at hand, opened a brisk fire that soon cleared the deck. Thus far, the Indian interpreter, from whom these particulars are derived, had been an eye witness to the deadly conflict. He had taken no part in it, and had been spared by the natives as being one of their race. In the confusion of the moment he took refuge with the rest, in the canoes. The survivors of the crew now sallied forth, and discharged some of the deck guns, which did great execution among the canoes, and drove all the savages to shore.

For the remainder of the day not an Indian ventured to put off to the ship, deterred by the effects of the fire-arms. The next day the Tonquin still lay at anchor in the bay, her sails all loose and flapping in the wind, and no one apparently on board of her. After a time, some of the canoes ventured forth to reconnoitre, taking with them the interpreter. They paddled about her, keeping cautiously at a distance, but growing more and more emboldened at seeing her quiet and lifeless. One man at length made his appearance on the deck, and was recognized by the interpreter, as Mr. Lewis. He made friendly signs, and invited them on board. It was long before they ventured to comply. Those who mounted the deck met with no opposition; no one was to be seen on board, for Mr. Lewis, after inviting them, had disappeared. Other canoes now pressed forward to board the prize; the decks were soon crowded, and the sides covered with clambering savages, all intent on plunder. These poor miscreants had supposed the Tonquin was theirs by right of possession; but in the midst of their eagerness and exultation, she blew up with a tremendous explosion. Arms, legs, and mutilated bodies were blown into the air, and dreadful havoc was made among the surrounding canoes. The interpreter was in the main chains at the time of the explosion, and was thrown unhurt into the water, when he succeeded in getting into one of the canoes. According to his statement, the bay presented an awful spectacle after the catastrophe. The ship had disappeared, but the bay was covered with fragments of the wreck, with shattered canoes, and Indians swimming for their lives, or struggling in the agonies of death; while those who had escaped the danger remained aghast and stupified, or made with frantic speed for the shore. Upwards of a hundred savages were destroyed by the explosion, many more were shockingly mutilated, and for days afterwards the limbs and bodies of the slain were thrown upon the beach by the waves. The inhabitants of Neweetee were overwhelmed with consternation at this astounding calamity, which had burst upon them in the very moment of triumph. The warriors sat mute and mournful, while the women filled the air with loud lamentations. Their weeping and wailing, however, was suddenly changed into yells of fury at the sight of four unfortunate white men, brought captive into the village. They had been driven ashore in one of the ship's boats, and taken on the beach. The interpreter was permitted to converse with them, and they proved to be the four brave fellows who had made such desperate defence from the cabin. The most of the particulars already related of this horrid tragedy, were gathered from them by the interpreter. They told him further, that after they had beaten off the enemy, and cleared the ship, Lewis advised that they should slip the cable and endeavor to get to sea. They declined taking his advice, alleging that the wind set too strongly into the bay, and would drive them on shore. They resolved, as soon as it was dark, to put off quietly into the ship's boat, which they would be enabled to do unperceived, and to coast along back to Astoria. They put their resolution into effect; but Lewis refused to accompany them, being disabled by his wound, hopeless of escape, and determined on a terrible revenge. On the voyage out, he had repeatedly expressed a presentiment that he should die by his own hands; thinking it highly probable that he should be engaged in some contest with the natives, and being resolved, in case of extremity, to commit suicide rather than be made a prisoner. He now declared his intention to remain on board of the ship till day-light, to decoy as many of the savages on board as possible, then set fire to the powder magazine, and terminate his life by a single act of vengeance. How well he succeeded has been shown. His companions bid him a melancholy adieu, and set off on their precarious expedition. They strove with might and main to get out of the bay, but found it impossible to weather a point of land, and were at length compelled to take shelter in a small cove, where they hoped to remain concealed until the wind should be more favorable. Exhausted by fatigue and watching, they fell into a sound sleep, and in that state were surprised by the savages. Better had it been for those unfortunate men, had they remained with Lewis, and shared his heroic death ; as it was, they perished in a more painful and protracted manner, being sacrificed by the natives to the manes of their friends with all the lingering tortures of savage cruelty. Some time after their death, the interpreter, who had remained a kind of prisoner at large, effected his escape, and brought the tidings to Astoria.

The loss of the Tonquin was a grievous blow to the infant establishment, and one that threatened to bring after it a train of disasters. The fate of her brave, but headstrong commander, and her adventurous crew, is a catastrophe that shows the importance of obeying instructions. It had been repeatedly enjoined upon Captain Thorn, by Mr. Astor, to be courteous and kind in his dealings with the savages, but by no means to confide in their apparent friendship, *nor to admit more than a few on board of his ship at a time.*

CHAPTER III.

Gloomy aspect of affairs at Astoria—Overland Expedition of Messrs. Hunt and McKenzie, &c.

The little colony now found themselves a mere handful of men, on a savage coast, surrounded by hostile tribes, who would doubtless be incited and encouraged to deeds of violence by the late fearful tragedy. Mr. McDougal had recourse to a stratagem by which to avail himself of the ignorance and credulity of the savages, which does credit to his ingenuity. The natives of the coast, and, indeed, of all the regions west of the mountains, had an extreme dread of the small-pox ; it having appeared among them several years before, and swept off entire tribes. They looked upon this scourge as an evil brought among them by the white men, or inflicted upon them by the Great Spirit. The former idea was seized upon by McDougal. He called together several of the chiefs whom he believed to be in the conspiracy, and informed them that he had heard of the fate of the Tonquin, and was determined on summary vengeance. "The white men among you" said he, "are few in number, it is true, but they are mighty in medicine. See here," continued he, drawing forth a small bottle and holding it before their eyes, "in this bottle I hold the small-pox, safely corked up; I have but to draw the cork, and let loose the pestilence, to sweep man, woman and child from the face of the earth." The assembly was struck with horror and alarm—implored him not to uncork the bottle, since they and all their people were firm friends of the white men, and would always remain so; but should the small-pox be once let out, it would sweep off the good as well as the bad; and surely he would not be so unjust as to punish his friends for crimes committed by his enemies. McDougal pretended to be convinced by their reasoning, and assured them that, so long as they were friendly and hospitable to the white people, the vial of wrath should remain sealed up; but on the slightest provocation, the fatal cork should be drawn. This strategy had the desired effect, and from this time he was much dreaded by the natives as one who held their fate in his hands, and was ever after called, by way of pre-eminence, "the Great Small-pox Chief." A permanent post being thus established at the mouth of the Columbia by the Pacific Fur Company, after many privations, hardships and disasters, we will recur to the overland expedition, under the superintendence of William Price Hunt.

This gentleman is represented as being scrupulously upright and faithful in his disposition, and of most accommodating manners, but unacquainted with Indian trade and warfare. Donald McKenzie was associated with Mr. Hunt in this expedition, and excelled in those points in which the other was deficient; for he had been ten years in the interior, in the service of the North-west Company, (British) and valued himself on his knowledge of "wood-craft," and Indian character. Messrs. Hunt and McKenzie accordingly repaired, about the latter part of June, 1810, to Montreal, where every thing requisite for such an undertaking could be procured. Here too, their first object was to recruit a complement of Canadian voyagers. Having completed their "outfit," they proceeded up the Ottawa river in a canoe, thirty or forty feet in length, and though capable of carrying a freight of upwards of four tons, could readily be carried on men's shoulders. They proceeded by the ancient route of the fur-traders, along a succession of small lakes and rivers, to Michilimackinac. The party arrived at Mackinac on the 22d of July, and here they increased their recruits till they numbered thirty, to which it had originally been limited; but it was now determined, before proceeding up the Missouri, to increase it to the number of sixty. On the 12th of August they left Mackinaw, and pursued the usual route by Green Bay, Fox and Wisconsin rivers, to Prairie du Chien, and thence down the Mississippi to St. Louis, where they landed on the 3d of September. At this place Mr. Hunt met with much opposition on the part of rival traders, especially the Missouri Fur Company, and it took him some weeks to complete his preparations. The delays here, and previously on the way, threw him much behind his original calculations, so that it was impossible for him to effect his voyage up the Missouri in the present year. He accordingly left St. Louis on the 21st of October, determined to push up the river as far as possible, to some point above the settlements where game was plenty, and where his whole party could be subsisted by hunting until the breaking up of the ice in the spring should permit them to resume their voyage. On the 16th of November they had made their way four hundred and fifty miles up the Missouri to the mouth of the Nodowa, and here they resolved to establish their winter quarters; and in fact, two days after they had come to a halt, the river closed just above their encampment. In January, 1811 Mr. Hunt left the encampment in charge of the other partners, and set off on foot for St. Louis, where he arrived on the 20th of the same month. His object was to obtain a re-inforcement of hunters, and also an interpreter acquainted with the Sioux language; as from all accounts he apprehended danger in passing through the country of that nation. April 17th Mr. Hunt returned with his party from below, and the rains having subsided, the winter encampment was broken up, and their course resumed up the Missouri. On the 28th they breakfasted on one the islands which lie at the mouth of the Nebraska, or Platte river; the largest tributary of the Missouri, and about six hundred miles above its confluence with the Mississippi. This point was originally established as the dividing line between the upper and lower Missouri; and the earlier voyagers in their toilsome ascent, before the introduction of steamboats, considered one-half of their labor accomplished, when they reached this place.   On the 10th of May the party arrived at the Omaha village, eight hundred and thirty miles above the Mississippi, where they remained till the 15th.   A few days after leaving this village, Mr. Hunt met three Kentucky hunters on ther return home.   Their names were Edward Robinson, John Hoback, and Jacob Rizner.   Here they were, a thousand miles from civilization, but in the midst of enjoyment.   Robinson was a veteran back-woodsman, sixty-six years of age.   He had been one of the first settlers of Kentucky, and engaged in many of the conflicts with the Indians on "the Bloody Ground." In one of these battles he had been *scalped*, and he still wore a handkerchief bound round his head to protect the part.   These men had passed several years in the upper wilderness.   They had been in the service of the Missouri Fur Company, and had crossed the Rocky Mountains the preceding year, after being driven from their post on the Missouri, by the hostility of the Blackfeet Indians.   They had remained on the head waters of the Columbia river, hunting and trapping, until having satisfied their wandering propensities, they felt disposed to return to the families and comfortable homes they had left in Kentucky.   They had accordingly made their way back across the mountains, and down the rivers, and were in full career for St. Louis, where they came across Mr. Hunt and his party.   The sight of a powerful company of trappers, traders and hunters, well armed and equipped, furnished at all points, in high health and spirits, and banqueting lustily on the green margin of the river, was a spectacle too stimulating for men of their natures.   When they come to learn the grand scope and extent of the enterprise in hand, it was irresistable : homes, wives and children, and all the charms of green Kentucky vanished from their thoughts ; they cast loose their canoes to drift down the stream, and turned their backs again to the east, and joyfully enlisted in the band of adventurers.   Such are the charms to which back-woodsmen are wedded.

In the afternoon of June 1st they arrived at the great bend of the Missouri river, where it winds for about thirty miles round a circular peninsula, the neck of which is not more than two thousand yards across.   The scenery and objects, as they proceeded, gave evidence that they were advancing deeper and deeper into the domains of savage nature.   Boundless wastes kept extending to the eye, more and more animated by herds of buffalo.   Sometimes these animals were seen moving in long processions across the silent landscape ; at other times they were scattered about singly or in groups, on the broad prairies and green hills. At one place the shores of the river seemed absolutely lined with them ; many were on their way across the stream, snorting, blowing and floundering. Numbers, in spite of every effort, were born by the rapid current within shot of the boats, and several were killed. At another place a number were seen on the beach of a small island, under shade of the trees, or standing in the water like cattle, to avoid flies and the heat of the day. Several of the best marksmen stationed themselves in the bow of a barge, which advanced slowly and silently, stemming the current with the aid of a broad sail and a fair breeze. The buffalo stood gazing quietly at the barge as it approached, perfectly unconscious of their danger. The fattest of the herd was selected by the hunters, who all fired together, and brought down their victim. Beside the buffaloes, they saw abundance of deer, and frequent gangs of stately elks, together with light troops of sprightly antelopes, the fleetest and most beautiful inhabitant of the prairies. There are two kinds of antelopes in these regions ; one nearly the size of the common deer, the other not much larger than a goat. Their color is a light gray, slightly spotted with white ; and they have small horns like those of the deer, which they never shed. Nothing can surpass the delicate and elegant finish of their limbs, in which lightness, elasticity, and strength, are wonderfully combined. Their habits are shy and capricious; they keep on the open prairie or plains, are quick to take the alarm, and bound away with a fleetness that defies pursuit. While they trust to their speed, they are safe ; but they have an itching curiosity that sometimes betrays them to their ruin. When they have scud for some distance, and left their pursuer behind, they will suddenly stop and turn to gaze at the object of their alarm. If the pursuit is not followed up, they will, after a time, yield to their inquisitiveness, and return to the place from whence they have been frightened. One of the party named John Day, an old hunter, showed his experience and skill in entrapping one of these beautiful animals. Taking advantage of its well known curiosity, he laid down flat among the grass, and putting his handkerchief on the end of his ramrod, waved it gently in the air. This had the fabled effect of fascination. The antelope gazed at the mysterious object for some time at a distance, then approached timidly, pausing and reconnoitring with increased curiosity ; moving round the point of attraction in a circle, but still drawing nearer and nearer, until being within range of the deadly rifle, he fell a victim to his curiosity.

On the 12th of June, Mr. Hunt and his companions arrived at the village of the Arickaras, situated between the 46th and 47th parallel of N. latitude, and fourteen hundred and thirty miles above the mouth of the Missouri. There they found one of those haphazard wights of French origin, who abound upon our frontier, living among the Indians like one of their own race. He had been twenty years among the Arickaras, had a squaw and a troop of piebald children, and officiated as interpreter to the chiefs. Messrs. Hunt and Mackenzie stopped at this place by invitation, attended a council lodge, had a *talk* with the chief of the village, and explained to the savages the nature of their voyage, and their intention of debarking there, and proceeding onward by land ; and that they would like to trade with them for a supply of horses for the journey. They landed amidst a rabble crowd, and were received by the chief, who conducted them into the village ; driving to the right and left swarms of old squaws, imp-like boys, and vagabond dogs, with which the place abounded. The cabins looked like dirt-heaps huddled together without any plan, filthy in the extreme, and prolific of villanous smells.

On the 18th of July, Mr. Hunt took up his line of march by land from this place, without being able to obtain a sufficient number of horses for the accommodation of all his people. His cavalcade consisted of eighty-two horses, most of them heavily laden with Indian goods, beaver-traps, Indian corn, ammunition, corn meal, and other necessaries. Each of the partners was mounted, and a horse was allotted to Pierre Dorion, the interpreter, for the transportation of his luggage and his two children, while his *squaw*, for the most part of the time, trudged on foot, with the residue of the party.

About the middle of September, the party had crossed the Rocky Mountains, among which they found deep ravines, — the head waters of rivers flowing into the Atlantic and Pacific. Their horses had dangerous falls in some of these places. One of them rolled, with his load, nearly two hundred feet down hill into the river, but without receiving any injury.

They had now conquered the chief difficulties of this great rocky barrier, and at their feet flowed the rapid current of Mad river, a stream ample enough to admit of the navigation of canoes. The *voyageurs* rejoiced at the idea of exchanging their horses for canoes, and of gliding down the bosoms of rivers, instead of scrambling over the backs of mountains. In the frightful wilderness that still intervened between them and the shores of the Pacific, they were yet to encounter many hardships and perils; but of them all, they were unmindful, and passed onward with courage and cheerfulness, till on the 21st of January, 1812, the wayworn travelers lifted up their eyes and saw before them the long sought waters of the Columbia. The sight was hailed with as much transport as though they had already reached the end of their pilgrimage; nor can we wonder at their joy. Their whole route by land and water since leaving the Arickara village on Missouri, had been, according to their computation, seventeen hundred and fifty-one miles, in the course of which they had endured all kinds of privations.

The place where they struck the Columbia was some distance below the junction of the two great branches, Lewis' and Clark's Rivers, and not far from the influx of the Wallah-Wallah. It was a beautiful stream, three-fourths of a mile wide at this place, totally free from trees, bordered in some places with steep rocks, in others with pebbled shores.

From this place the party continued their journey, alternately by land and water, and were much delayed by the straying of the horses, and the attempts made by the Indians to steal them. They frequently passed Indian lodges where they obtained fish and dogs, for food. At one place the Indians had just returned from hunting, and had brought back a large quantity of elk and deer meat, but asked so high a price for it as to be beyond the funds of the travelers; so they had to content themselves with dog flesh. They had by this time, however, come to consider it very choice food, superior to horse flesh, and the minutes of the expedition speak rather exultingly now and then, of their having made a " famous repast," where this viand happened to be unusually plenty.

The country, in general, in the neighborhood of the river, was a continual plain, low near the water, but rising gradually. In a few days they came to where the country became hilly and the river made its way between rocky banks, and down numerous rapids. The Indians in this vicinity were better clad and altogether in more prosperous condition than those above, and showed their consciousness of ease by something like sauciness of manner. Thus prosperity is apt to produce arrogance in savage as well as in civilized life. In both conditions, man is an animal that will not bear pampering.

From these people Mr. Hunt for the first time obtained vague but deeply interesting intelligence of that part of the enterprise which had proceeded by sea to the mouth of the Columbia. The Indians spoke of a number of white men who had built a large house at the mouth of the great river, and surrounded it with palisades. None of them had seen it; but rumors spread widely and rapidly from mouth to mouth among the Indian tribes, and were carried to the heart of the interior, by hunting parties and migrating hordes.

The establishment of a trading emporium at such a point, also, was calculated to cause a sensation to the most remote parts of the wilderness beyond the mountains. It, in a measure, struck the pulse of the great vital river, and vibrated up all its tributary streams.

It was surprising to notice how well this remote tribe of savages had learnt through intermediate gossips, the private feelings of the colonists of Astoria; for they told Mr. Hunt that the white people at the large house had been looking anxiously for many of their friends, whom they expected would descend the great river; and had been in much affliction, fearing that they were lost.

January 31st, they arrived at the falls of the Columbia, and encamped at the village of Wish-ram, situated at the head of that dangerous pass of the river called "the Long Narrows."

This village was the great Indian fishing mart of the Columbia; here the tribes from the mountains resorted to trade; and the inhabitants were more shrewd and intelligent than their neighbors. Traffic had sharpened their wits, though it had not improved their honesty; for they were a community of arrant rogues and free-booters. The party would have gladly departed from this thievish neighborhood on the day of their arrival; but were detained by violent head winds, accompanied with snow and rain, and also in procuring the requisite number of canoes to transport them to the mouth. As it was, they left on the 5th of February, and, on the afternoon of the 15th, swept round an intervening cape, and came in sight of the infant settlement of Astoria. As might naturally be supposed, a shout of joy burst from each canoe at the long wished for sight. The day was given up to jubilee, to celebrate the arrival of Mr. Hunt and his companions, and the joyful meeting of the various scattered bands of adventurers at Astoria. The colors were hoisted; the guns, great and small, were fired; there was a feast of fish, of

beaver, and of venison, which relished well with men who had
so long been glad to revel on horse flesh and dog's meat ; a liberal
allowance of grog was issued to increase the general animation,
and the festivities wound up, as usual, with a grand dance at night
by the Canadian voyageurs.

The distance from St. Louis to Astoria, by the route traveled
by Hunt and McKenzie, was about three thousand five hundred
miles, though in a direct line it does not exceed half that distance.

Having traced the fortunes of the two expeditions by sea and
land, to the mouth of the Columbia, we will dwell for a moment
on the history of the colony, from this time to the 16th of October, 1813, when the fort, furs, and merchandise of all kinds,
passed into the hands of the British. In the course of the summer
and autumn of 1811, the Pacific Fur Company had established
quite a number of trading posts in the interior of the country,
the principal of which was situated at the confluence of the Okanagan river with the Columbia, four hundred miles above Astoria.   As yet, Mr. Astor had heard nothing of the success or ill-
luck of the previous expeditions, and adhered to his first intentions
by sending out to the colonists the annual ship, freighted with a
cargo for the factory.   The ship Beaver, of four hundred and
ninety tons, commanded by Captain Sowle, sailed from New York
on the 10th of October, 1811, on board of which embarked a
re-inforcement of a partner, five clerks, fifteen American labor-
ers, and six Canadian voyageurs.   Captain Sowle was instructed
to touch at the Sandwich Islands, inquire about the fortunes of
the Tonquin, and whether an establishment had been formed at
the mouth of the Columbia.   If so, he was to take as many
Sandwich Islanders as his ship would accommodate, and proceed
thither.   On arriving at the river, he was to observe great caution, for even if an establishment should have been formed, it
might have fallen into hostile hands.   He was, therefore, to put
in as if by casualty or distress, to give himself out as a coasting
trader, and to say nothing about his ship being owned by Mr. Astor, until he had ascertained that every thing was right.   He received the same injunctions that had been given to Captain Thorn,
of great caution and circumspection in his intercourse with the
natives, and that he should not permit more than one or two to be
on board at a time.

The Beaver reached the Sandwich Islands without any occurrence of moment, and here the rumor was first heard of the disastrous fate of the Tonquin.   Deep solicitude was felt by every

one on board, for the fate of both expeditions, by sea and land. Doubts were entertained whether any establishment had been formed at the mouth of the Columbia, or whether any of the company would be found there. After much deliberation, the Captain took twelve Sandwich Islanders, for the service of the factory, should there be one in existence, and proceeded on his voyage.

On the 6th of May, 1812, he arrived off the mouth of the Columbia, and running as near as possible, fired two signal guns. No answer was returned, nor was there any signal to be descried. Night coming on, the ship stood out to sea, and every heart drooped as the land faded away. On the following morning they again ran within four miles of shore, and fired other signal guns, but still without reply. A boat was then despatched, to sound the channel, and attempt an entrance ; but returned without success, there being a tremendous swell, and breakers. Signal guns were fired again at evening, but equally in vain, and once more the ship stood out to sea for the night. The captain now gave up all hope of finding any establishment at the place, and indulged in the most gloomy apprehensions. He feared his predecessors had been massacred before they reached their place of destination ; or if they should have erected a factory, that it had been surprised and destroyed by the natives. In this moment of doubt and uncertainty, John Clarke, the partner on board, announced his determination, in case of the worst, to found an establishment with the present party, and all hands bravely engaged to stand by him in the undertaking. The next morning the ship stood in for the third time, and fired three guns, but with little hope of reply. To the great joy of the crew, three distinct guns were heard in answer. The apprehensions of all but Captain Sowle were now at rest. That cautious commander recollected the instructions given him, and determined to proceed with great circumspection. He was well aware of Indian treachery and cunning. It was not impossible, he observed, that these cannon might have been fired by the savages themselves. They might have surprised the fort, massacred its inmates ; and these signal guns might only be decoys to lure him across the bar, that they might have a chance of cutting him off, and seizing his vessel.

At length the white flag was seen hoisted as a signal on Cape Disappointment. The passengers pointed to it in triumph, but the Captain did not yet dismiss his doubts. A beacon fire was struck up at night on the same place, but the captain remarked that all these signals might be treacherous.

On the morning of May 9th, the vessel came to anchor off Cape Disappointment, outside of the bar. Towards noon an Indian canoe was seen making for the ship, and all hands were ordered to be on the alert. A few moments afterwards, a barge was perceived following the canoe. The hopes and fears of those on board the ship, were in tumultuous agitation, as the boat drew nigh that was to let them know the fortunes of the enterprise, and the fate of their predecessors. The captain, who was haunted with the idea of possible treachery, did not suffer his curiosity to get the better of his caution, but ordered a party of his men under arms to receive the visitors. The canoe came first alongside, in which was Comcomly, a chief, and six Indians ; in the barge, the familiar face of Duncan McDougal was recognised, and a little conversation soon dispelled all the captain's fears, and the Beaver crossing the bar under their pilotage, anchored safely in Baker's Bay.

Soon after the arrival of the Beaver, Mr. Hunt, the general agent of the company, determined to proceed in her to visit the Russian settlements farther to the north, for the purpose of arranging commercial transactions with them. He accordingly left Astoria in August, for this purpose, leaving the factory in charge of Mr. McDougal.

In January, 1813, news reached the fort that war had been declared by the United States against Great Britain, and in June following, a partner of the North-West Company (British) arrived from Canada, with the report of an approaching English naval force, to take possession of the mouth of the Columbia. This information was received with manifestations of pleasure by McDougal, and a considerable proportion of the persons in the employ of the Pacific Fur Company, who were Scotchmen and Canadians, too many of whom had been in the employ of the North-West Company. Several trappers immediately left the Pacific Company and joined the North-West Company again, and others determined to abandon the enterprise, unless assistance should soon arrive from New York. Notwithstanding the gloomy state of affairs, Mr. Astor determined to send another ship to the relief of the settlement ; and selected for this purpose, a vessel called the Lark, remarkable for her fast sailing. The disordered state of the times caused such delay that she did not put to sea till the beginning of March, 1813. The officer who was to command her shrunk from his engagement, and in the exigency of the moment, she was given in charge to Mr. Northrop, the mate. Nicholas G. Ogden went in her, as supercargo ; but unfortunately this ship never reached Astoria, being wrecked on one of the Sandwich Islands. When within a few degrees of these islands, a gale sprang up that soon blew with tremendous violence. The Lark was a staunch and noble ship, and for a time buffeted bravely with the storm. Unluckily, however, she " broached to," and was struck by a heavy sea, that hove her on her beam ends. The helm, too, was knocked to leeward, all command of the vessel was lost, and another mountain wave completely overset her. Orders were given to cut away the masts, and unfortunately, in the hurry and confusion, the boats also were cut adrift. The wreck then righted, but was a mere hulk, full of water, with a heavy sea washing over her, and all the hatches off. On mustering the crew, one man was missing, who was discovered below in the forecastle, drowned. In cutting away the masts, it had been utterly impossible to observe the necessary precaution of commencing with the lee rigging, that being, from the position of the ship, completely under water. The masts and spars therefore remained fastened to the wreck for four days, and during this time, the ship lay rolling in the trough of the sea, the heavy surges breaking over her, and the spars heaving and banging to and fro, bruising the half-drowned sailors that clung to the bowsprit and the stumps of the masts. The sufferings of these poor fellows were intolerable.

The first mate soon died at his post, and was swept off by the surges. Three days after, two seamen, faint and exhausted, were washed overboard. The next wave threw their bodies back upon the deck, where they remained washing backward and forward, ghastly objects to the almost perishing survivors. Mr. Ogden, the supercargo, who was at the bowsprit, called to the men nearest to the bodies to fasten them to the wreck, as a last horrible resource in case of being driven to extremity by famine ! As the gale died away, the sailors crawled feebly about the deck, cleared away the spars, threw the anchors and guns overboard ; the spritsail yard was rigged for a jury-mast, and a mizzen topsail set upon it. There was a Sandwich Islander on board, an expert swimmer, who found his way into the cabin, and occasionally brought up a few bottles of wine and porter. A little raw pork was likewise procured, and dealt out with a sparing hand. The horrors of their situation were increased by the sight of numerous sharks prowling about the wreck, as if waiting for their prey. A week after the gale had subsided, the cook, a black man, died, and was cast into the sea, when he was instantly seized upon by these ravenous monsters. Some of the natives, soon after, came alongside in their canoes, with a most welcome supply of potatoes. Captain Northrop was convinced that the only chance for their lives was to get to land in the canoes, and stand ready to receive and protect the wreck when it should drift ashore. They landed on the small, inhospitable island called Tahoorowa, and in the course of the night, the Lark came drifting to the strand, with the surf thundering around her, and shortly afterwards bilged. The sagacious Tamehameha, king of the islands, agreed to furnish the men with provisions so long as they remained; but showed himself an experienced *wrecker*, by insisting that the vessel with its cargo should be abandoned to him as a waif, cast by fortune on his shores.

The United States Government had determined this year, to send the frigate Adams to the North Pacific, for the protection of the settlement at the mouth of the Columbia, but when ready to sail from New York, it was found necessary to transfer her crew to Lake Ontario.

On the 7th of October, 1813, a party belonging to the British fur traders arrived at Astoria, commanded by Messrs. McTavish and Stuart, and brought information that the North-West Company had fitted out a large armed ship at London, which was then on its way to the Columbia, with the design of seizing and destroying every thing American which they could find on the North-West Coast.

At the same time they proposed to purchase the whole of the establishments, furs, goods and property of the Pacific Company, at a fair valuation. The posts at this time belonging to the Pacific Company were Astoria, Okanagan, Spokan House, one in the Flat Head country, one on the Kooskooskie river, and one on the Wallamette. The proposition was accepted by Mr. McDougal, and on the 16th of October a contract was signed, by which the furs and merchandise of all kinds belonging to the company, passed into the hands of the North-West Company for $40,000, in bills on Montreal, while the actual worth of the property sold was over $100,000. The following estimate was afterwards made of the articles on hand, and the prices paid for them: —

17,705 lbs. beaver parchment sold	for	$2,00	worth		$5,00
465 old coat beaver	"	" 1,66	"		3,50
907 land otter skins	"	" 50	"		5,00
68 sea otter skins	"	" 12,00	" 45 or		50,00
30 do. do.	"	" 5,00	"		25,00

For the following articles no allowance was made : —

179 mink skins, worth each	....	$0,40
22 racoon	"	"	 40
38 lynx	"	"	 2,00
18 fox	"	"	 1,00
106 do.	"	"	 1,50
71 black bear	"	"	 4,00
16 grizzly bear	"	"	 10,00

Scarcely had the agreement been executed, when the British sloop of war Racoon, Captain Black, entered the Columbia, hoping to reap a rich harvest, but was greatly disappointed. He only had the honor of lowering the United States flag which was still waving over the factory, and hoisting that of Britain. *With all the solemnity the occasion required*, Captain Black gave to Astoria, the name of Fort George.

During Mr. Hunt's absence to the Russian settlements, he learned that a war was going on between England and the United States, and that a British force was on the way to the mouth of the Columbia. He proceeded to the Sandwich Islands, chartered the American brig Pedlar, with which he sailed for Astoria, for the purpose of conveying the property of the company to Canton. He did not arrive there till the 28th of February, 1814. He found McDougal still in charge of the factory, *but as an agent and partner of another firm*, and Mr. Hunt having received the bills given in exchange for the company's effects, re-embarked in the Pedlar, and proceeded to the United States via China.

But for the occurrence of these unforeseen circumstances, there is no doubt but that the enterprise might have been successful, and the United States at this time been in quiet and undisturbed possession of the whole of Oregon.

CHAPTER IV.

History of operations in the Territory since the last War with England. Description of the country—its rivers, harbors, towns, trading posts, animals, climate, resources, &c. &c., interspersed with a summary of important facts.

Whilst the Hudson's Bay Company has been prosecuting its operations with the greatest activity, the citizens of the United States have been comparatively idle. For some considerable time after the breaking up of Mr. Astor's Pacific Fur Company, few American citizens made their way to this region ; although an extensive trade was carried on east of the Rocky Mountains, principally by the North American Company, of which Mr. Astor was at the head.

In the year 1823, Mr. W. H. Ashley, of St. Louis, projected an expedition to the country beyond the Mountains ; and in the course of that year, crossed the ridge with a party, near the 42d degree of latitude, and procured a large quantity of furs, with which he returned to St. Louis. In the succeeding year, he again crossed the Rocky Mountains, and left a party of about a hundred hunters and trappers in that country. This party, although obliged to contend against the efforts of the Hudson's Bay Company, succeeded in collecting furs, to the value of 180,000 dollars, in the course of three years. In these early expeditions, the goods, designed for the purchase of furs, were transported from St. Louis, on horses ; but since then, wagons have usually been employed, for transporting the merchandise to the foot of the mountains, and sometimes across the mountains, by the *southern pass*, near the 42d parallel of latitude ; and it is said, that a light carriage has been driven from Connecticut, to the falls of the Columbia, 125 miles from the Pacific.

In 1826, the interest of Mr. Ashley was united with that of other merchants of St. Louis, under the name of the Rocky Mountain Fur Company : which carried on a regular trade with the countries drained by the Colorada and Columbia. About this time, too, the North American Fur Company extended its operations beyond the Rocky Mountains, and collected large quantities of furs.

In 1832, Captain Bonneville, of the United States army, conduct d a party, consisting of about a hundred men, with twenty wagons, to the country in the vicinity of Lewis River; where they remained two years, engaged in hunting, trapping, and trading with the Indians.*

About the year 1833, Mr. Nathaniel Wyeth, of Massachusetts, projected a plan for carrying on a direct trade between the Atlantic ports of the United States, and the Columbia, by which merchandise, suitable for the Indian trade, should be exchanged for furs and salmon.

He accordingly sent a vessel around to the coast, and two parties by land, across the mountains, and established a trading post, called Fort Hall, on Lewis River, near the confluence of the Portneuf; and another, on Wappatoo Island, at the junction of the Wallamet with the Columbia, sixty miles from the ocean.

On account of the continual opposition of the Hudson's Bay Company, he was eventually obliged to abandon his enterprise.†

Since that period, parties from the United States occasionally cross the Rocky Mountains, and carry on a small traffic with the natives; but no extensive operations of that kind have been recently engaged in, by citizens of the United States. The United States has no "mammoth corporation," like the British Hudson's Bay Company, and no private association of traders can enter into competition with that company, with the slightest chance of success. Hence our trade with that territory has diminished —the fur trade is almost altogether shut out from our citizens— and all this by the British construction of the terms of the Convention of 1818, and 1827, which gives to British subjects the same right to hunt, fish, &c., that our own citizens possess; but no right to establish permanent settlements, or military posts. That British subjects have done so, is evident from the statements, under the head of the operations of the Hudson's Bay Company.

The following extract of a letter from Messrs. Smith, Jackson and Sublette to the Secretary of War of the United States, gives an account of the first expedition with wagons to the Rocky Mountains :—

"On the 10th of April last, (1829) we set out from St. Louis, with eighty-one men, all mounted on mules, and ten wagons, each drawn by five mules, and two dearborns, each drawn by one

---

* The Adventures of Captain Bonneville, by Washington Irving.

† See Report to the House of Representatives, Feb., 1839.

mule.   Our route was nearly due west, to the western limits of
the State of Missouri, and thence along the Santa Fe trail; a-
bout forty miles from which, the course was some degrees north
of west, across the waters of the Kansas, and up the Great Platte
River, to the Rocky Mountains, and to the head of Wind River,
where it issues from the mountains.   This took us until the 16th
of July, and was as far as we wished the wagons to go ; as the
furs to be brought in, were to be collected at this place, which is,
or was this year, the great rendezvous, of the persons engaged
in that business.   Here the wagons could easily have crossed the
Rocky Mountains, it being what is called the *southern pass*, had
it been desirable for them to do so ; which it was not, for the
reason stated.

"For our support, at leaving the Missouri Settlements, until
we should get into the buffalo country, we drove twelve head of
cattle, besides a milch cow.   Eight only of these being required
for use before we got to the buffaloes, the others went on to the
head of Wind River.   We began to fall in with the buffaloes, on
the Platte, about 350 miles from the white settlements : and from
that time lived on buffaloes ; the quantity being infinitely beyond what we needed.   On the 4th of August, the wagons being
in the meantime, loaded with the furs which had been previously
taken, we set out on the return to St. Louis.   All the high points
of the mountains then in view, were white with snow ; but the
passes and valleys, and all the level country, were green with
grass.

"Our route back, was over the same ground nearly, as in going out ; and we arrived at St. Louis, on the 10th of October,
bringing back the ten wagons : the dearborn being left behind.
Four of the oxen, and milch cow, were also brought back to the
settlements in Missouri, as we did not need them for provision.
Our men were all healthy, during the whole time.   We suffered
nothing by the Indians, and had no accident but the death of one
man being buried under a bank of earth that fell in upon him,
and another being crippled at the same time.

"Of the mules, we lost but one by fatigue, and two horses,
stolen by the Kanzas Indians ; the grass being along the whole
route, going and coming, sufficient for the support of the horses
and mules.   The usual weight in the wagons, was about 1800
pounds.   The usual progress of the wagons was from fifteen to
twenty-five miles per day.   The country being almost all open,
level and prairie, the chief obstructions, were ravines and creeks;

the banks of which, required cutting down : and for this purpose, a few pioneers were generally kept ahead of the caravan. This is the first time that wagons ever went to the Rocky Mountains, and the case and and safety with which it was done, prove the facility of communicating over land, with the Pacific Ocean ; the route from the Southern Pass, where the wagons stopped, to the Great Falls of the Columbia, being easier and better than on this side of the mountains, with grass enough for horses and mules, but a scarcity of game, for the support of men."

In going from the United States, the traveller enters the south eastern limits of Oregon Territory, at the northern extremity of Bear river valleys, and in looking over the country it is found to possess many important rivers and harbors, that, considering their intimate relation to the general interest of commerce, seem to demand our first attention.

The Columbia and its branches water almost the entire territory, and open a highway from the ocean to the lofty mountain ranges which form its eastern boundary. This river heads in lat. 52° north. long. 119° west from Greenwich, and after persuing a serpentine course for fifteen hundred or two thousand miles, finds its discharge in the Pacific, at lat. 46° north.

One hundred and twenty miles of this distance are navigable for ships of the largest class, but the remainder of its course is interrupted by occasional rapids and falls, that render frequent portages necessary.

The upper and lower "dalls" and "cascades," present the most serious impediments to navigation. The former of these, situated above Clarke's Fork, are caused by the passage of the Columbia through immense ledges, that leave huge vertical walls of basaltic rock upon either side, and compress its waters to a narnow, chasm-like channel. There, dashing and foaming in wild fury, the torrent rushes past its lateral dikes with frightful velocity.

The distance between these two "dalls" is some thirty miles.

The "cascades" lie at the base of a mountain range of the same name, one hundred and fifty miles from the Ocean. Near this place the whole stream is plunged over a precipice of fifty feet descent, forming a sublime and magnificent spectacle.

Between the dalls and cascades, a reach of high-lands, formed almost entirely of naked basalt, presents another barrier, through which the river forces itself by a tunnel-like pass for ten or fifteen miles, leaving vast mural piles upon the right and left, that attain an altitude of three hundred and fifty or four hundred feet.

A few miles above the junction of the southern and middle forks of the Columbia, two considerable lakes have been formed by the compressure of its waters among the adjoining mountains.

The first of these is about twenty miles long and six broad, shut in by high, towering hills, covered with stately pine forests.

Emerging from this, the river urges its way through lofty embankments of volcanic rock for some five miles or more, when a second lake is formed in a similar manner, which is about twenty-five miles in length and six in width.

There are also several other lakes, of greater or less extent, at different points along its course.

Perhaps no river in the world, of the same length, affords such varied and picturesque scenery as does the Columbia.

Its lakes, tunnels, cascades, falls, mountains, rocky embankments, prairies, plains, bottoms, meadows, and islands, disclose an agreeable medley of wild romance, solemn grandeur, and pleasing beauty, far surpassing that of any other country.

During its course it receives numerous tributaries, the most important of which are the Clarke, Flat-bow, Spokan, Okanagan, Snake, Yakama, Piscous, Entyatecoom, Umatilla, Quisnel, John Day, D'Chute, Cathlatates, Wallawalla, Wallamet, and Cawlitz.

The Clarke, Snake, and Wallamet rivers, seem to call for more than a bare allusion.

The former of these rises in the Rocky Mountains, near latitude 46° north, and following its windings, is about five hundred and fifty miles in length. A lake, some thirty miles long and eight broad, is also formed in its course, about one hundred miles above its mouth. During its windings it receives a large number of affluents, which unite to swell the volume of its waters to the full size of its parent stream.

Note.—Capt. Fremont, in speaking of the Columbia, makes use of the following just observations:

"The Columbia is the only river which traverses the whole breadth of the country, breaking through all the ranges, and entering into the sea. Drawing its waters from a section of ten degrees of latitude in the Rocky Mountains, which are collected into one stream by three main forks (Lewis', Clarke's, and the North Fork) near the sea, while its three forks lead each to a pass in the mountains, which opens the way into the interior of the continent.

"This fact, in reference to the rivers of this region, gives an immense value to the Columbia. Its mouth is the only inlet and outlet to and from the sea: its three forks lead to passes in the mountains; it is, therefore, the only line of communication between the Pacific and the interior of North America; and all operations of war or commerce, of national or social intercourse, must be conducted upon it."

The Snake, or Lewis' Fork, is equally important. It rises in latitude 42° north, and, pursuing a north-westerly direction for five hundred miles, is discharged into the Columbia, in latitude 46° north. This river also receives several tributaries, the largest of which are the Kooskooskie and Salmon.

The Wallamet heads in the Cascade Mountains, in Upper California, near latitude 41° north, and bears a northerly course for nearly three hundred and fifty miles. One hundred and twenty-five miles of this distance are navigable for boats of a light draught.

Several tributaries, both from the east and west, unite to increase its magnitude and enhance its importance.

The Umpqua, which is the next river worthy of notice below the Columbia, has its source in the Cascade Mountains, near latitude 43° north, and running a westerly direction for almost three hundred miles, is finally discharged into the Pacific. This stream is said to be navigable for some forty or fifty miles of this distance.

A short distance south of the Umpqua a stream of nearly equal size empties into the Pacific, called Rogue's river. This also rises in the Cascade Mountains, at latitude 42° north, and is said to be navigable for boats of a light draught, for some seventy miles or more.

The Chilkeelis is the first river north of the Columbia, and rises in the mountains, near latitude 48° north. Pursuing a westerly course, it discharges itself into the Pacific at Gray's Harbor, after flowing a distance of about two hundred and fifty miles.

Fraser's River is the extreme northern one of Oregon. It heads in the Rocky Mountains, near latitude 54° north, and empties into the Gulf of Georgia, in latitude 49° north. In its course it receives several large tributaries, and pursues its way for a distance of about four hundred miles, eighty of which are navigable.

Besides those above named, there are several other streams, of less magnitude, emptying into the Pacific at various points above its coast, all of which, as the country becomes settled, will contribute to the facilities of commerce and manufactures.

The rivers of Oregon, in the abundance and quality of their fish, are unparalleled. At certain seasons of the year, their waters are completely alive with the countless myriads that swarm them to their very sources.

Even the small streams are not exempt from this thronging population.   So great is the number, they are frequently taken by the hand; and, with the aid of a net, several barrels may be caught at a single haul. It requires but little effort to obtain them, and large quantities are annually shipped to the Sandwich Islands and various other points.

Fish are undoubtedly destined to furnish an important item in the future commerce of Oregon.   At the present time they supply the principal food of its inhabitants, both Indians and whites. Among the different varieties abounding in these streams, salmon and salmon-trout claim the precedence, both in numbers and qualities.

These delicious fish attain a size seldom surpassed, and are found in every accessible river and creek. The bays, harbors, and mouths of rivers are also thronged with cod, herring, sturgeon, and occasionally whales, while vast quantities of oysters, clams, lobsters, &c., may be obtained along the coast.

Next to fish, in connection with the rivers, the extraordinary number of aquatic birds arrests the attention. These consist of geese, brants, ducks (of three or four varieties,) swans, pelicans, and gulls.

At certain seasons, they throng the rivers, creeks, lakes, and ponds, at different parts, in innumerable multitudes, and not only keep the waters in constant turmoil from their nautic exercises and sports, but fill the air with the wild clamor of their incessant quackings. An expert sportsman may kill hundreds of them in a few hours.

So abundant are they that their feathers may be obtained of the Indians in any requisite quantity, for a trifling consideration—in all respects equal, for bedding, to those procured from domesticated geese and ducks.

In regard to harbors, the natural advantages of Oregon are not equal to those of California; though, as the country becomes settled, the ingenuity of man will speedily atone for these apparent deficiencies; and if she has not the matchless basin of the Bay of San Francisco, she has other localities upon her seaboard that, with a small expenditure of money and effort, may be made secure and adapted to all her commercial requirements.

It is much to be regretted, however, that the Columbia affords not an easy and secure entrance for ships from the Ocean, as this will undoubtedly become the most important point of the whole coast.

At present, the mouth of this river, between Points Adams and Hancock, is partially blocked up by large sand-bars, deposited by the current, and maintained in their places through the repulsive action of the sea-waves.

How far these impediments may operate to the future detriment of commerce, remains to be seen. Unless some remedy should be adopted, the harbor of this great embryo depot of Western trade will continue to oppose a difficult entrance.

The estuaries of the Umpqua and Rogue rivers are more difficult of access than the Columbia. It is even said, that there is not a good harbor on the coast of Oregon below lat. 46° north. Above this parallel there are several, not only easy of access but secure of anchorage; the principal of which are those of the Straits of Juan de Fuca and the Gulf of Georgia. The islands of Vancouver and Queen Charlotte* also possess a number of excellent harbors.

These islands are large, well timbered, and generally fertile. Though, like the main land, quite broken and hilly, they embrace many beautiful plains and lovely valleys, abounding with game, and coursed by ample streams of fresh water. Vancouver's Island is two hundred and sixty miles long by fifty in width, and Queen Charlotte's one hundred and forty by twenty-eight. In addition to the above named, there are a number of smaller islands near the Straits of Juan de Fuca—more important on account of their fisheries than the quality of their soil.

The Rocky Mountains, forming its eastern boundary, branch off westerly and northwesterly at various points, and, in connection with other ridges, beline the whole country. It is my present purpose merely to classify some the more extensive of these ranges, and note their locality, as auxiliary to a more accurate and comprehensive disposal of the leading subject before the reader.

The Blue Mountain chain commences not far from 45° 30′ north latitude, and bears a southerly course, till it passes into California and unites with the interesting ridges of that province.—It runs nearly parallel with the Rocky Mountains, at an interval varying from one hundred to one hundred and fifty miles, forming the Eastern Division of Oregon.

---

*By the terms of the late treaty, the islands of Vancouver and Queen Charlotte are transferred to Great Britain, leaving only a few diminutive and comparatively valueless ports in the Straits of Juan de Fuca and in islets south of Vancouver, within the limits of the U. S. territory.

The Cascade chain (before noticed, in connection with California) commences in the Russian possessions, and pursues a southerly course through both countries, till it finally becomes lost in the sea-girt isthmus of the Lower Province. It runs parallel with the coast, at a distance varying from one hundred to one hundred and fifty miles, and defines the Western and Middle Division of Oregon.

The country north of the Columbia is also traversed by numerous branches and spurs of the Rocky and Cascade Mountains, many of them presenting lofty peaks, covered with never-melting snow and ice.

The mountain ranges before described, have many summits towering far above the snow-line. They are generally less sterile than the main chain of the Rocky Mountains, and, amid their snow-clad tops and denuded eminences, present alternate spreads of high table land and rolling prairie, clothed with vegetation, and dense forests of pine, cedar, fir, and oak, or opening valleys arrayed in all the enchantment of vernal loveliness.

The Eastern, or Southeasterly Division of Oregon, partakes of a greater variety of wild and savage scenery, intermixed with beauty and desolation, than any other section in the whole territory.

The valleys of Bear river and those parts contiguous to Fort Hall, have already been described on a preceding page, and all their varied attractions fully descanted upon. Besides these, there are other valleys in the neighborhood of the South Pass, upon Little and Big Sandy, and the New Forks of Green river, that claim a passing notice.

The valleys last referred to are of variable width and possess a fertile soil, adapted to either grazing or agricultural purposes, and assume an additional importance from their situation in reference to the grand routes from the United States to Oregon and California. They are capable of sustaining a small population with peculiar advantage, were it not for the troubles that might be anticipated from the hostile incursions of the Blackfeet and Sioux.

Below Fort Hall, the valleys of Snake, or Lewis' river, are somewhat limited, but very fertile, though enclosed for the most part by denuded and sterile mountains. In the vicinity of Fort Boise, on the bank of Lewis' Fork, are several rich and extensive plains and valleys, more or less adapted to cultivation.

The Kooskooskie and Salmon rivers, also, present some fine bottoms. Another beautiful valley is situated upon Powder river, a considerable creek. about forty miles below Fort Boise. It is large and very fertile, but lacks a sufficiency of timber without a resort to the dense pine forests of the neighboring hills.

The next section that attracts the traveler's attention as he proceeds towards the Columbia, is a favored spot known as *le Grand Rond*, bounded on all sides by mountains, in the vicinity of the Blue range. This locality is nearly circular, and about one hundred and fifty miles in circumference, well watered and possesses a soil of matchless fertility. Timber of the best kind may be procured, in any quantity, from the adjoining mountains, and, to a limited extent, from the valley.

Trappers speak of the *Grand Rond* with an enthusiasm which is cordially responded to by all who have hitherto visited it. So far as soil and climate are concerned, a better section of country than this is rarely found.

South-east from the place last described, sixty miles or more, lies a long stretch of desolate country, which bears a strikingly volcanic appearance.

This region is thickly paved with vast piles of lava and igneous rock, strown about in confused fragments, as if the mountains had been rent asunder and dashed in horrid medley upon the adjoining plains, and earth, itself, had undergone all the indescribable contortions of more than agony,—now opening in frightful chasms,—now vibrating with unheard-of violence, oversetting hills and rooting them from their foundations by the impetuosity of its motion, or elevating half vertically, the immense layers of subterranean rock forming the valves of distorted fissures. and depressing the opposing ones in frightful contrast,—in haste to complete the picture of destruction by an imposing array of wild and savage scenery.

Numerous boiling springs are also found among the widespread heaps of ruined nature whose waters are frequently so hot that meat may be cooked in a very few minutes by submersion in them.

Several streams trace their way through this region, affording occasional bottoms of fertile soil and luxuriant vegetation, that smile with bewitching enchantment upon the relentless havoc surrounding them.

Upon Clarke's River and its tributaries, as well as the numerous lakes adjacent to them, there are large quantities of excellent land, well adapted to agricultural and grazing purposes. The hills, too, are generally studded with dense forests of pine and fir, some of them of gigantic growth, while the intervening plateaux and high rolling prairies present frequent intervals of lusty grasses.

The same may be said, though in a more restricted sense, of most of the country lying between Clarke's River and the Columbia.

The streams of water and lakes are most of them skirted with bottoms and valleys of greater or less extent, tolerably well timbered, while the neighboring hills afford frequent groves of heavy pines, diversified with openings of grass-clad prairies or of denuded barrenness.

Many interesting localities lie along the Columbia, above the confluence of Clarke's River, as well as upon the several tributaries finding their way into it. A tract of country circumjacent to the Lower Lake possesses a rich soil, with other advantages, which in due time will command the attention of emigrants.

The section lying still north of this is but little better than a barren waste of frost and snow, with now and then choice spots of rank vegetation and rich floral beauty, shut up in their stern recesses, in wonderful contrast with the savage sublimity and wild disorder of the masses of naked rock that surround them.

Fraser's River has an extensive valley of excellent and well timbered land, skirting it in variable width, from mouth to source. The same may be said of many of its tributaries. The Chilkeelis, also, possesses many choice spots.

But, as a general thing, that portion of the country north of the Columbia is the most worthless part of Oregon.

A vast share of it is mere naked rock or deserts of ice and snow, with now and then dense forests of pine, cedar, and fir. There are, comparatively, few arable prairies ; and not more than one-half of the whole extent can be turned to any useful purpose. Perhaps one-sixth of it is susceptible of cultivation. In fact, the only localities worthy of mention are the valleys scattered among the Claset and Cascade Mountains, and along the different rivers and creeks.

The cause of this general sterility is more to be attributed to the severity of the climate, consequent upon a high northern latitude, combined with the broken and mountainous character of the country, than to any great natural deficiency of soil. Of course it can never become thickly populated.

Its timber, fisheries, and facilities for manufactures, stock-raising, and the growth of wool, embrace its greatest inducements to emigrants; though, in a commercial point of view, its extensive fur trade and commodious harbors, with other kindred advantages, should not be overlooked.

We now come to the Middle Division, or that section south of the Columbia, between the Blue and Cascade Mountains.

In this division of Oregon the face of the country is very much diversified. As a whole, it presents a continued series of conical hills, huge masses of rock, and undulating prairies, intermixed with lofty, cloud-capped peaks, shooting transversely from the ridges that form its eastern and western boundaries. These mountains are usually clothed with rank vegetation, and frequently present stately forests of valuable timber, particularly the Blue range.

It also contains many extensive valleys of great fertility, situated among its mountains, and upon the John Day, Quisnell, Umatilla, D'Chute, and Wallawalla Rivers, and their numerous affluents.

The southern extremity likewise affords many fertile and extensive valleys, but it is rather sparsely timbered. In the immediate vicinity of the Columbia, the land is sandy and barren, though back from the river, the hills are tolerably rich, and coated with heavy pine forests.

Nearly the whole of this section may be considered available for agriculture and stock-raising.

The Western Division next commands our attention. Below the Cascades, the country contiguous to the Columbia presents a vast extent of thickly timbered and extremely fertile bottom land, one hundred and twenty miles wide, interspersed with frequent openings of lusty vegetation.

The forests of this section afford some of the largest and most beautiful pine and fir trees in the world. Its valleys, plains, and hills are likewise possessed of a most excellent soil, adapted to every practicable use.

Above this, and bordering upon the Straits of Juan de Fuca, are also large tracts of fine land, well watered, timbered, and fertile.

Southward, towards the confines of California, the Umpqua and Rogue Rivers claim several very extensive and fertile valleys and bottom lands. Upon the former of these are said to be two, one of which is forty miles in length by ten in width, and the other about seventy by fifteen;—upon the latter, is one eighty miles long, and varying from fifteen to fifty in width.

Besides those above mentioned, there are numerous other valleys, all of which are well timbered and of unparalleled fertility.

No country in the world affords a better soil, or more romantic scenery.   The mountains bounding them rise in stately grandeur, oftentimes far above the clouds, to converse with the relentless snows of successive ages,—now presenting their nude sides, paved with dark masses of frowning rocks, or proud forests of evergreen, verdant lawns, flowery dales, and steril wastes, to overlook the perennial beauty and matchless fecundity at their feet,—while the lesser eminences, with their deep ravines, o'erhanging cliffs, and shadowy recesses, tell the place where the storm-winds recruit their forces and the zephyrs creep in to die.

There are also large valleys, of equally fertile soil, upon the head waters of the Tlameth river, near the southern boundary, well worth the attention of emigrants.

The most interesting portion of the Western Division, however, is that bordering upon the Wallamet and its affluents.   The valley of this river is one hundred and fifty miles long by about thirty-five broad.   The soil is a deep alluvion, of extraordinary fertility.

It is not only well watered, but well timbered, and produces all the vegetables, fruits, and grasses indigenous to the country, with astonishing profuseness.   No region was ever better adapted to agricultural or grazing purposes.

The Fualitine Plains, adjoining this beautiful expanse of fertility upon the left, towards the Columbia, embrace an area of forty-five miles in length by fifteen in breadth, well watered and amply timbered, with a soil in all respects equal.

The Klackamus, Putin, Fualitine, Yamhill, and other rivers, are all of them skirted by beautiful and fertile valleys of greater or less extent, while the adjacent hills and prairies afford not only frequent forests of excellent timber, but generally a very good soil.

The landscape of this vicinity, though not, strictly speaking, hilly, is highly undulating, but quite productive in grass and herbage.

The Cawlitz river, which empties into the Columbia a short distance below the Wallamet, has several rich bottoms, and waters a large extent of country, admirably adapted to stock-raising and agriculture.

At the mouth of the Wallamet river is an island some fifteen miles in length by nearly the same distance in breadth, called Wappatoo ; it is of a deep alluvial soil, formed from sedimentary deposits and decayed vegetable substances, and is very rich and densely timbered.

The country at the mouth of the Columbia and for some ten or fifteen miles interior, in sandy and steril,—a fact much to be regretted, as from its peculiar locality this point must necessarily become the site of a vastly important commercial emporium, vieing in population, splendor, and opulence, with the time-grown cities of more eastern climes.

The stately forests of pine and fir, in the Western Division of Oregon, have for a long time challenged the admiration of the world, and it is strongly doubted whether the chosen veterans of foreign woods can produce a rival to some few specimens of the proud giants of its soil.

These not unfrequently tower to a height of two hundred feet, and even more,—leaving from one hundred and fifty to one hundred and seventy-five feet clear of limb, with scarcely a curve in the entire length.

One of them, standing near Fort George on the Columbia, is said to measure forty-seven feet in circumference, three hundred and fifty feet in altitude, and two hundred and sixty-five feet clear of limb ; another, upon the Umpqua river, is reported even larger, and yet another, in the same vicinity, very nearly equals it in size.

Timber of this kind affords the choicest article for lumber, which bears a very high price in the Sandwich Islands and in various parts of Mexico, and will no doubt become a staple commodity in the commerce of Oregon ; while the immense forests of pine, fir, and oak, rearing their stately heads in thick array, must prove a source of wealth to its future inhabitants.

The principal kinds of wood indigenous to the country are white-oak, live-oak, sugar-maple, ash, pine, fir, cedar, hemlock, spruce, cottonwood, aspen, and cherry.

Live-oak is found chiefly in the southern part, and, in quality, stands foremost among the denizens of the forest for ship building. Several other species of oak are more or less abundant in various parts.

A mountainous country like this must necessarily embrace

every variety of climate, from that of the ice-bound coasts and
ever-scathing frosts of the polar regions, to the burning heat of
the equator,—from the mild atmosphere of Italian skies, to the
genial temperature which paints the wild-flowers in their primeval beauty, while month succeeding month doles out the year,
nor feels nor knows the chill-breath of winter.

A short jaunt at any time translates the traveler, at his own
option, to regions of winter, spring, summer, or fall, and spreads
before him all the varied beauties and deformities of cither.

As a general thing, however, the winters of Oregon are much
more temperate than those of countries in the same latitude bordering upon the Atlantic—a fact which may be attributed to the
usual prevalence of westerly winds at that season.

These winds, on passing the mountains and traversing the vast
extent of snowy prairie and open land in their course, become
vested with a chilling severity unknown to its incipiency, when,
from the warm bosom of the broad Pacific, they first waft themselves o'er the blooming valleys, smiling plains, grass-clad hills,
and mountains garbed in stately forests, commingled with stern
desolation, to lavish upon all these varied scenes the soft bland-
ishments of the Indies, and engender the interesting phenome-
non of a southern climate in a high northern latitude.

The country contiguous to Fraser's river, and even below it
for some distance, is usually visited with long and severe winters, and enjoys comparatively but a short interval of genial
weather during the spring and summer months.

The valleys, however, not unfrequently afford exceptions to
this remark, when favorably located in regard to the wind and
sun. In this section it seldom rains, a circumstance causing an
unproductive and arid soil.

The Eastern Division is, perhaps, more variable in regard to
temperature than any other portion of Oregon. Its valleys are
usually possessed of a mild and delightful climate, so much so
that stock will subsist the entire winter without being fed or
housed.

The plains and high prairies present a longer interval of in-
clement weather, and the snow continues on the ground for a
much greater length of time, than in the low-lands.

Some particular localities are subject to very sudden changes,
and not unfrequently experience the warm breath of summer
with the chill blasts of fresh-born winter during the short lapse
of a single day and night.

In reference to the high mountains, it is sufficient to remark, that with them winter is a season too congenial not to be felt in all its rigors, to the entire extent of its duration. The diversity of temperature in these parts depends mostly upon the altitude. The lower benches experiencing a mild atmosphere even in the severest weather, permit the snow to remain only for a short interval succeeding its fall, and woo the willing spring ; while the higher ones treasure up each descending flake to nourish the scathing blasts that leap from the mountain-tops, fresh-cradled in the lap of winter.

Notwithstanding these apparent disadvantages, the Eastern Division may be regarded as universally healthy. The purity of the atmoshere, and its absence from noxious exhalations and disease-engendering effluvia, undoubtedly contribute the prime cause in producing a result so favorable.

Rains are not usual to this part in the summer months, nor even in the winter and spring are they common to any great extent. The snows of winter, together with the rains of that season and autumn, and the occasional dews of summer, in most cases, afford a sufficient moisture to the low-lands for agricultural purposes.

That section situated between the Blue and Cascade Mountains, known as the Middle Division, is said to possess, comparatively, a much milder and less variable climate.

The winters are usually open and of short duration, snow lying upon the ground, in the valleys, rarely exceeding four days in succession, and vegetation, in some instances, remains green the entire season. The prairies, too, are generally covered only for a short time.

The heat of summer lacks that oppressiveness so common to most countries. In regard to the health of this section, we may correctly apply the observations made relative to the Eastern Division. A country situated like the one now forming the subject of our remarks, cannot be otherwise than healthy, as a general thing.

The snow of winter and the rains of spring and autumn, coupled with the light dews of summer, furnish all the moisture usual to the soil, which the moderate heat of the latter season renders sufficient for the growth of vegetation and the production of grain and other crops.

The Western Division possesses not only a soil but a climate more favorable to vegetation than any other portion of Oregon.

In the southern part it seldom snows, and the weather is so mild, that the grass continues green and flourishing the entire year. Water never freezes, unless it be in some elevated pool or lake.

The absence of sufficient rains and dews, however. during the summer months at some points, renders an occasional resort to irrigation necessary for the production of corn, potatoes, and articles of a like nature.

Two crops of some kinds of produce may be raised with success in a single year.

In the vicinity of the Wallamet, the winters are only a trifle colder. Running water seldom freezes. Snow never falls to exceed the depth of a few inches, and disappears in a very short time succeeding.

Vegetation in the valleys, and even upon the plains, to some extent, remains green year in and year out. Of course no better climate could be selected for stock-raising.

These remarks may be applied with equal propriety to the other portions of the Western Division south of the Columbia and in its immediate vicinity. The country further north, for a considerable distance, possesses a climate almost as favorable. The snows of winter, however, are usually more frequent and less transitory in their continuance.

The cold season is confined almost exclusively to the three winter months. The heat of summer is moderate and agreeable, generally ranging at 62° Fahrenheit, above zero, in its mean temperature.

The wet season of the Western Division usually occurs from October to March of each year, inclusive ; at other times rain seldom falls. During this season it descends in gentle showers, or in the shape of mist, at intervals, for about one half of the time. The moisture received into the earth meanwhile, together with the nightly dews and other favorable agencies during the summer months, renders the soil adapted to cultivation.

Back from the valleys and bottoms, the atmosphere is quite wholesome and salubrious. Fevers are seldom known, and pulmonary complaints are equally rare.

In the vicinity of the Columbia, intermittent fevers are not uncommon, though by no means as bad as in some parts of our frontier States.

The soil and climate of the Eastern Division have been sufficiently tested to know their capacity for producing nearly, if not quite, all the various grains, vegetables, and fruits usually grown in our Northern and Middle States. A great variety of wild fruits and vegetables grow spontaneously, in different parts, and in great abundance.

The soil and climate, as a whole, seem better adapted to the culture of fruits and grains, than vegetables; and perhaps we might add, for the raising of cattle, horses, and sheep, than agriculture; though the latter observation is not to be so construed as to affirm that farming may not be successfully and profitably prosecuted in many parts.

The Northern Division, or that portion of Oregon lying on the head-waters of the Columbia, in the vicinity and south of Fraser's river, and upon the Chilkeelis, being much colder and more sterile, must necessarily be regarded in a less favorable light than the country referred to in the preceding paragraph. But, little is known as to its products or the capacities of its soil and climate; yet, it is said that some particular kinds of fruit are indigenous to this region, and it is generally supposed that wheat, barley, oats, buckwheat, flax, and other articles of like nature, might be raised within it. Of course, these remarks apply only to the valleys.

The Middle Division affords a finer soil and a more favorable climate than the Eastern; but, in regard to productions, it is much the same. All the northern fruits, grains, and vegetables, may be produced in great abundance, with the exception of corn —the land being generally too dry and too much subject to unseasonable frosts; corn, however, has been successfully cultivated on the Wallawalla.

There are several varieties of wild fruits found here, among which are included cherries, with larb, buffalo, goose, and service berries, and currants, plums, and grapes, together with several other species, as well as vegetables and roots.

The Western Division not only maintains its pre-eminence in relation to soil and climate, but stands equally conspicuous in the variety and abundance of its productions. It is thought, and not without reason, that cotton, sugar-cane, and various other productions of a warm and even tropical climate might here be raised without difficulty.

When the ground is in a suitable condition, the avarage crop of wheat is from twenty to twenty-five bushels to the acre. Vast quanti.ies of it are annually produced by settlers in different parts of the country. A surplus of one hundred thousand bushels is reported to have been grown, in the region adjoining the Wallamet, during the summer of 1844.

The Hudson's Bay Company, at Fort Vancouver, have several very extensive farms under improvement, upon which they raise nearly every variety of grain and vegetables, with flattering success.

In the garden of McLaughlin, the chief factor of this company, are found almost every species of fruits and flowers indigenous to this country and to foreign soils of the same latitude, with several varieties produced only in warm climates.

We barely allude to the above facts, in order to prove the adaption of Western Oregon to agricultural pursuits. The data relative to its extraordinary facilities for rearing countless herds of cattle, horses, and sheep, have already been placed before the reader, and need not here a repetition.

The components of the soils of Oregon are equally varied in character, according to their situation. The bottoms are usually of a deep, sandy alluvion, itermixed with vegetable and organic matter. The valleys are of a heavy loam, enriched by the debris and other fertilizing properties borne from the high grounds by the annual rains, together with the constant accumulation of decayed herbage and grass so lavishly bestrown at each returning season.

The prairies are possessed of either a light sandy superfice, or a mixture of gravel and stiff clay. The superstratum of the hills and mountains varies from wastes of naked sand, sun-baked clay, aud spreads of denuded rock, to a thin vegetable mould, and a light marly loam of greater or less fecundity.

The rock of this territory also presents many different specimens ; the prominent classifications, however, are volcanic, viz: basalt, (columnar and scoriated,) trap, lava, pumicestone, limestone (fossiliferous, bituminous, and earthly,) and mica slate, with sandstone, puddingstone, granular quartz, calcarious tufa, and agglomerated boulders of various kinds, particularly in the Eastern Division. The varieties of some parts present strong characteristics of the oolite formation. The hills contain many excellent quarries for the structure of buildings or other useful purposes.

Hitherto but little investigation has been had relative to the mineral resources of Oregon ; though sufficient is known to warrant the statement, that copper, lead, iron, coal, salt, soda, sulphur, nitre, and alum, are abundant in some parts ; and, from the nature of the country, we may safely infer that yet more valuable metals are waiting to reward with their hidden treasures the researches of man.

Game, in the Eastern and Middle Divisions, is not generally plentiful ; yet, in places, there are an abundance of deer, elk, antelope, bear, wolves, and foxes ;—buffalo are also found occasionally in the vicinity of the Rocky Mountains. In the Northern Division, moose, deer, elk, bear, foxes, and wolves, are the varieties most common. Game is more abundant in the Western than in the other Divisions, and is nearly of the same kind.

Ducks, geese, pheasants, partridges, &c., are common throughout the whole territory.

Wolves are very numerous in the neighborhood of the settlements, and prove a great source of annoyance to the inhabitants by preying upon their cattle and other stock. These wolves consist of three kinds,—the black, gray, and prairie wolf, of which, as in California, the black wolf is the largest and most ferocious.

As a grazing country, the available lands of the three divisions of Oregon, south of the Columbia. and the one immediately north of that river, are little inferior, if, indeed, not fully equal, to the far-famed meadows and lawns of California.

Horses are reared in vast numbers by the Indians, among whom it is not uncommon to find a single individual owning three or four hundred head. Select horses may be bought at prices ranging from twelve to twenty dollars each.

These horses are generally stout and hardy, capable of enduring a vast amount of fatigue, and are but little inferior in point of size to our American nags.

Large herds of horses are also raised by the settlers, and at the Hudson's Bay Company's establishments.

Latterly, cattle, hogs, and sheep, are beginning to receive the attention of the farming community, and, without doubt, soon will become immensely numerous. It needs only the operation of time to render Oregon as famous for its countless herds, as for the abundance and variety of its productions.

The entire population of the territory at this time, may be estimated at thirty-five thousand, of which about seven thousand are whites, and the balance Indians.

The Indians principally consist of the following tribes : The Snakes, Blackfeet, Flatheads, Nesperces, Bonarks, Cyuses, Wallawallas, Chinooks, Shatchets, Chalams, Killamucs, Squamishes,

Clasets, Tonados, Klackamus, Clatsup, Umpquas, Klackatats, Kallapuyas, Tlamaths, and Chilkeelis.

The Blackfeet, though included among the Oregon tribes, properly belong to that portion of the Rocky Mountains contiguous to the head waters of the Missouri. They make occasional irruptions into the country occupied by the Flatheads. Snakes, and Nesperces, and for this reason are included in the above list.

Tlamaths and two or three other inferior tribes in the neighborhood of California and north of the Columbia river may be considered troublesome and rather ill-disposed ; but not dangerous, unless it be in cases where they have a very decided advantage.

The Indians of this country are less warlike than those east of the Rocky Mountains, and far less dangerous, even as enemies. They may be considered, on the whole, as friendly to the whites, and quite susceptible of civilization. They are tolerably industrious, and ready at all times to work for the settlers at a trifling compensation.

Many of them cultivate the ground and raise corn, potatoes, beans, and melons,—but fish, horses, and game, as a general thing, furnish their principal food. As an evidence of their quiet disposition, they rarely go to war, and are usually found at or near the several places claimed and occupied by them individually.

The Nesperces are, perhaps, farther advanced in civilization than any other tribe. Many of them (and some of other tribes) are beginning to live after the manner of the whites, and the philanthropic efforts of Christian missionaries in their behalf have been attended with great success.

There are eight or more missionary stations in Oregon, belonging as follows : to the Presbyterians, the Methodists, and the Roman Catholics.

Four of these are situated between the Blue and Cascade Mountains, viz : one near the Dalls one at Waiilatpu on the Wallawalla, one at Tshimakain, and one at Clear Water.

The mission at Waiilatpu is under the direction of Dr. Whitman, and has a flourishing mill and a very considerable farm connected with it, upon which large quantities of grain and vegetables are annually raised, and also numerous herds of cattle and horses. The station near the Dalls, with the exception of a mill, is said to be but little behind that of Waiilatpu in point of prosperity.

The remaining four are in the Western Division.

The most importrnt of these are situated as follows : one at the Wallamet Falls, about twenty-five miles below the Columbia, and the other in the Wallamet valley, some forty or fifty miles farther south.

Both of the above belong to the Methodists, and may be considered rich.

There are two large farms and a store connected with the station in the Wallamet valley, and also large heids of cattle, horses, and hogs ;—it is said to drive quite a profitable trade with the Indiana and settlers in the line of dry goods and groceries.

The station at the Wallamet Falls has also a store, and carries on a small business by way of merchandize.

The two other stations are south and west of the last named, but have, as yet, no very extensive improvements in connection with them.

The Methodists have a press at one of their stations in Oregon, which is employed in printing religious books for the benefit of the Indians.

In addition to the different stations above alluded to, the Catholics have several agents and teachers in this territory, who labor with great zeal and earnestness to make proselytes to their own peculiar notions.   The number and locality of these agents I have not the necessary information to state.   They were, not long since, under the superintendnece of one Father De Smit, a Jesuit priest, and have exerted considerable influence among the Indian tribes.

Nearly the entire trade of Oregon, at the present time, is in the hands of the Hudson's Bay Company, from whom dry goods and groceries may be obtained by the settlers at less than the common price in the United States ; this, as a necessary consequence, precludes all opposition.   The principal exports (raised at the stations or received by way of barter) are flour, fish, butter, cheese, lumber, masts, spars, furs, and skins.

The Forts, or trading establishments, are eighteen in all, and have a large number of hands employed about them, in conducting the fur trade and laboring upon the farms and in the workshops and mills.

Each of these posts presents a miniature town by itself, whose busy populace pursue most of the varied avocations incident to the more densely inhabited localities of civilized countries.

We will not occupy the reader's time in an extended description of them severally, but rest content by simply giving their names. The first post belonging to this company, upon tho route to the mouth of the Columbia, is Fort Hall; the next, Fort Wallawalla; then, Fort Vancouver, and Fort George.

The others are situated at different points, and are known as follows: Colville, Okanagan, Alexandria, Barbine, Klamloops, St. James, Chilcothin, Simpson, McLaughlin, Langley, Nisqually, Cawlitz, and Umpqua; of which eight are located in or above lat 49° north.

The principal settlements, disconnected from the trading establishments and different missionary stations, at present, are upon the Umpqua and Wallamet rivers, on the Fualitine Plains, and near Fort Vancouver. These settlements are represented as being in a very flourishing condition, and rapidly increasing in population and wealth.

At the Wallamet Falls, a town has been regularly laid out called Oregon City, which, in the year 1844, numbered a hundred or more houses; among them was a church, with several stores and mills.

At this place the temporary legislature, already instituted by the settlers for mutual benefit in the absence of all other legitimate jurisdiction, holds its regular session. A mayor was elected in the spring of 1845; and recently a printing press and materials have been procured from New York for the purpose of publishing the territorial laws, with such other documents and papers as the interests of the community may require.

This embryo city, situated as it is in a place so admirable in regard to agriculture, commerce, and manufactures, possesses many superior advantages in point of locality.

The falls of the Wallamet are thirty feet perpendicular, and afford abundant water privileges for mills and factories,—two important rivers, the Klackamus and Fualitine, find their discharge near it, while below is presented an uninterrupted navigation to the Ocean, and above it boats may ascend for a distance of one hundred miles or more. The country contiguous is unsurpassed in fertility, and will undoubtedly soon acquire a dense population.

Another town, called Linnton, has recently been commenced upon the south bank of the Columbia, near the mouth of the Wallamet river, and bids fair to become of some importance.

The settlements in the valley above, and at the Fualitine Plains, are scattered like those of the farming sections of our

Western States;—the same observation may also be applied in reference to those upon the Umpqua river.

The settlement at Vancouver is more compact, and assumes the air of a flourishing village. It is near the falls of the Columbia, at the head of ship navigation, and is made the great commercial depot of the Hudson's Bay Company for the articles required in their trade.

Connected with the Fort is an extensive flouring mill, and also a saw-mill, which is said to do a very active and lucrative business.

The number of buildings at Vancouver is not far from sixty. The site is a most admirable one for some future emporium of trade and manufactures. Its water privileges are almost without limits, while its other advantages are equally inviting.

The geographical condition of the country is such that, as it becomes settled, an enormous amount of commercial interest must necessarily concentrate here; and doubtless, a more favorable locality for a city could not be selected upon the Columbia. It is destined to command almost the entire trade of Eastern and Middle Oregon.

The agents of the Hudson's Bay Company at present are of great advantage to emigrants. They extend to them every reasonable assistance by selling goods and necessaries on credit at very low prices, and receiving their various products in payment upon most favorable terms. They furnish seed-corn, wheat, potatoes, and other articles of like nature, to the settlers, to be returned in kind at the end of the year, with a small additional amount by way of interest.

This company is equally accommodating in other respects. It affords employment to numbers at a fair compensation, and supplies them with cattle, hogs, horses, and implements of agriculture for their farms. Its agents and factors seem much disposed to encourage the influx of emigrants, and are never backward in evincing a friendly disposition by their acts.

Perhaps no country is possessed of greater manufacturing facilities than Oregon. Its numberless watercourses, with their frequent falls and rapids, upon every side, point out the sites for mills and factories, while the adjoining forests and hills produce the timber for their construction, and the metal for their machinery; and the plains and valleys, the food for their operatives, and raw materials for their fabrics. The ships of all nations a-wait as their carriers, and render accessible the best markets of the world.

A large portion of the steril and otherwise valueless lands of the territory might be turned to good account in the growth of wool, and the valleys and bottoms would easily yield exhaustless supplies of flax and hemp. The southwest displays her cotton fields, and the plains and hills hold out their rich stores of timber and minerals; the busy operatives and thrice effective machinery of the flourishing establishments, as yet scarcely hidden from view by the thin veil of futurity, would achieve the transformation of these varied products into broadcloths, linens, calicoes, and other auxiliaries of comfort and utility; while California, with th.; other provinces of Mexico, the western Republics of South America, the islands of the Pacific, the Northwestern Coast, and the numerous Indian tribes of the interior, impatient to gaze upon the evidences of creative skill, even now stand their willing purchasers.

With such advantages before her, who might not augur well for the future pre-eminence of Oregon.

But, in other respects. the prospect is still more flattering. Her extensive plains, valleys, and bottoms, need no long lapse of time to transform them into smiling fields; her prairies and hills will then become thronged with countless herds of cattle and flocks of sheep, and the beef, pork, and wool of the stock-grower, butter and cheese of the dairyman, with all the surplus of the farmer, will find an inviting market at the populous manufacturing towns and commercial cities that will have sprung up close around him, nor need he look elsewhere for a more lucrative disposal.

An interchange of commodities with China, Japan, South America, the East Indies, and the Polynesian and Australian islands, will pour the wealth of nations into her lap, and swell the opulence of her citizens.

A continuous rail-road, from the Mississippi and the great lakes across the Rocky Mountains to the falls of the Columbia, (a project quite practicable, and even now seriously contemplated,) will open a new channel for commerce, and then our merchantmen and whalers, instead of performing a dangerous homeward-bound voyage of twelve thousand miles, by doubling the southern extremity of Africa, or that of the American continent, will discharge their cargoes at the ports of Oregon for a re-shipment to every part of the Union, and thus unite their aid in the magic work of up-building the Great West.

It is then that the mighty resources of our national confederacy will begin more fully to develop themselves, and exhibit to an admiring world the giant strides of civilization and improvement, when liberty is their birthright, and freemen their nursing fathers. It needs no prophetic eye to foresee all *this*, nor the effort of centuries to transform this rough sketch of fancy into a more than sober reality.

The overland route, from Independence, Mo., to Fort Hall, affords a good wagon-road ; but that from Fort Hall to Vancouver is generally considered impassable for other than pack-animals. It is said, however, that a new route has recently been discovered, by which wagons may be taken, without much difficulty, the entire distance. Should this report prove true, the emigrant may convey everything needed for his comfort during the long journey before him.

Emigrants should never go in companies exceeding one hundred and fifty or two hundred persons. The reason for this is obvious,—they will proceed more harmoniously ; there will be less difficulty in obtaining food for their animals ; less delays *en route* ; a better opportunity for the procurement of provisions by hunting, and the number is amply sufficient for mutual defence.

From my own experience and observation, I would advise the use of pack-mules, or horses altogether, instead of wagons. One pack-horse, suitably laden, would convey an ample supply of provisions and other necessaries for two individuals, if recruited by occasional levies upon the game that, in many cases, throng their course.

A company thus equipped, can travel with far greater expedition and even more comfortably.

In case of sickness, a litter might easily be constructed for the conveyance of the invalid by affixing to a horse two light poles, some twelve or fifteen feet in length, like the shafts of a wagon, the smaller extremities being fastened to the saddle and the larger ones let to drag upon the ground, while two short pieces placed transversely upon them, astern the horse, present the framework for a bed in which the sufferer may repose or lie at his ease, with as much quiet as the tender object of a mother's care in its infantile cradle.

A company acting upon the above suggestions (numbering say two hundred) should employ an efficient pilot, with a commandant and sixteen skilful hunters.

Strict regulations for its government must also be adopted and enforced. Each individual should be furnished with a good riding horse or a mule, a good percussion rifle, (bore thirty or thirty-five balls per lb.) ammunition sufficient for five hundred rounds, and a butcher-knife, with pistols and the requisites for procuring fire.

The company should be divided into messes of six each, and one hunter and his assistant should be assigned to every two messes. Each mess should be provided with three pack-mules, exclusively for the transportation of its baggage and provision, and at least one loose animal for extra service.

It should be further furnished with two camp-kettles, a tomahawk, a large tin mess-pan, and a tin cup and plate for each of its number.

A light tent might also be taken if deemed necessary ; though such an article is of little use. A robe and a blanket for bedding, four shirts and a single change of clothes are as much baggage as any individual should think of taking for his own use. By these means his movements will be free and unencumbered, while the whole company pursues its way with ease and rapidity.

On reaching his destination, the emigrant may procure every thing in the line of dry goods, groceries, and the implements of husbandry, at less prices than in the States ; hence the folly of burthening himself with extra baggage for a long and tiresome journey.

Fort Hall is situated upon the left bank of Lewis', or Snake river, in the south-eastern part of the territory, and in a rich bottom, near the confluence of the Pontneuf, in longitude 112° 20' 54" W., and latitude 43° 10' 30" N. It corresponds in its structure with most of the other trading establishments in the country. It was built in 1832, by Captain Wythe, of Boston, for the purpose of furnishing trappers with the needful supplies to exchange for beaver and other peltries, and also to command the trade with the Snake Indians.

Subsequently it was transferred to the Hudson's Bay Company, in whose hands it has since remained.

The following incident connected with its early history, tends to illustrate the bold daring, and spirit of inbred *republicanism,* possessed by the American hunters frequenting the mountains.

Soon after this post came into the possession of its present owners, several squads, on returning from their regular hunts, rendezvoused in its vicinity. According to the custom of the Hudson's Bay Company on such occasions, the British flag was hoisted in honor of the event. Thereupon the proud mountaineers took umbrage, and forthwith sent a deputation to solicit from the commandant its removal ; and, in case he should prove unwilling to comply, politely requesting that, at least, the American flag might be permitted a place by its side. Both of which propositions were peremptorily refused.

Another deputation was then sent announcing that, unless the British flag was taken down and the *stars and stripes* raised in its place within two hours, they would take it down by force, if necessary. To this was returned an answer of surly defiance.

At the expiration of the time named, the resolute trappers, mustering *en masse*, appeared before the fort, under arms, and demanded its immediate surrender.

The gates had already been closed, and the summons was answered by a shot from the bastion. Several shots were forthwith exchanged, but without much damage upon either side ; the trappers directing their aim principally at the British flag, while the garrison, feeling ill-disposed to shoot down their own friends in honor of a few yards of parti-colored bunting, elevated their pieces and discharged them into the air.

The result was that the assailants soon forced an entrance, took down and tore in pieces the hated flag, and mounted that of their own country in its stead, amid deafening huzzas and successive rounds of riflery.

The commandant and his sub-cronies, retreating to a room, barricaded the entrance, when the trappers promptly demanded their surrender upon the following terms :

1. The American flag shall occupy its proper place hereafter.
2. The commandant shall treat his captors to the best liquors in his possession.
3. Unless the offenders comply with these conditions, the captors will consider Fort Hall and its contents as lawful plunder, and act accordingly.

After a short parley, the besieged agreed to a capitulation. In compliance with the second article of the terms, a barrel of whiskey, with sugar to match, was rolled into the yard, where the head was knocked out, and the short but bloodless campaign was ended in wild frolicking, as toast after toast was drunk in fancied honor of the American flag, and round after round of responsive

cheers told who were they that stood ever ready to proudly hail
it and rally beneath its broad folds.

CHAPTER V.

The Grizzly Bear of the Rocky Mountains—his ferocity—instances of being
encountered by the hunters and trappers. The first Marriage Ceremony
over peformed in Oregon, in which a white person was interested—the parties concerned, &c.,—conclusion of the whole matter.

THERE are four varieties of bear found in the Rocky Mountains, and countries adjacent,—the grizzly bear. the white, the
red, and the black. Of these, the grizzly bear stands pre-emi-
nent in ferocity and strength. He will generally flee at the sight
or scent of a man. and seldom attacks any one unless wounded.
When shot, he almost invariably runs at full speed towards the
spot from whence the sound comes, and wo to the unfortunate
hunter who then comes in his way, unless fully prepared for a
deadly encounter. This animal reigns prince of the mountains,
and every other beast within his wide realm acknowledges his su-
premacy and pays him homage. Wolves and panthers dare not
approach him, or dispute the ti le of any thing. to which he lays
claim. Even the carcase of his prey, covered with the earth
and rocks, which his cautious instinct teaches him to heap upon
it, is unmolested, though hundreds of vagabond wolves and panthers might be fasting around. From the nature of these animals, we leave the reader to judge, whether their *moral honesty*,
or fear of vengeance, would be most likely to subdue their thievish propensities, when hungry.

A buffalo dreads his presence far more than the dangerous approach of the hunter, and will sooner bring into requisition their
swiftest powers of flight on such occasions. With great difficulty
a horse can be persuaded to go within any near distance of one
of the n, even when led, and then he will quail and tremble in
every joint, from extreme terror. In short, the grizzly bear stalks
forth at pleasure in his majesty and strength, undisputed monarch
of the wild solitudes in which he dwells, and no one dares oppose
him. Some natural historians have asserted that bears will not
prey upon dead carcases ; but hunters have known them to devour with avidity, the flesh of animals when nearly putrid. They

frequently kill buffalo, horses, and cattle, to gratify their propensity for animal food ; and, in such cases, they always drag their prey to some convenient spot, and perform the task of inhumation by heaping upon it piles of rock or earth, to a depth of several feet, for protection against the voracity of other beasts of prey. It is not uncommon, even, that they drag the entire carcase of a full-grown bull a distance of several yards, by the horns or tail, for this purpose,—so great is their strength and acute their sagacity.

Many stories, of thrilling interest, are related of frightful encounters with the grizzly bear, and the following one is none the worse for being somewhat comical.

A few years since, a trapper having set his " grappling irons" over night, returned to examine them in the morning, and, to his surprise, one of them was missing. After cautiously surveying the premises, under the impression that some renegade Indian had stolen his trap with its contents, he noticed the tracks of bears near by, which served at once to unravel the mystery of its abduction.

He now began to muse upon his loss, as, without the missing trap, his set would be rendered incomplete ; and, under present circumstances, the want of the thing greatly overbalanced the worth of it. While thus ruminating, a slight noise among the neighboring cherry bushes caught his ear, which sounded like some one beating with two sticks. This induced him to approach for the purpose of ascertaining the cause ; when an opening revealed to view a bear seated upon a log, and holding to his face the missing trap, tightly clasped to his fore-paw. Mr. Bruin appeared to be regarding the strange instrument with close and scrutinizing attention, as if endeavoring to fully investigate the principles of its construction,—now gazing at it endwise, then bringing its side in close proximity to his eyes ; then turning it over to examine the opposite side ;—now, he would essay its strength, and slightly taps it upon the log. But this last is a painful operation,—he relinquishes it and resumes his former baboon-like movements. Watching this curious performance, the trapper could scarcely retain his gravity, or master his love of the ludicrous sufficiently for the intended shot. He did, however, and the comedy was suddenly transformed, *a la Shakspeare*, to a tragedy, by leaving its actor struggling in death.

An excellent hunter, who had lived in the Rocky Mountains for several years, had imbibed the *habit* of letting no opportunity of killing any one of the various species of bear, common to those regions, pass unimproved. Never did he think of fearing them, and was always the last to retreat in case of a charge. When a bear appeared within any reasonable shooting distance of our hunter, it almost invariably fell a victim to his unerring aim. But, ere long, this spirit of temerity proved the source of lasting regret to its possessor.

On one occasion, having shot at one of these animals, contrary to his usual good luck, he only wounded it. The bear in turn now became the assailant, but received the contents of two pistols before it had time to advance far. Our hunter at this crisis of the warfare, sprang to a neighboring tree, which he commenced climbing. His pursuer, gaining the tree almost as soon, likewise began his ascent.

Here occurred a struggle between them,—the man to force his way upwards, and the bear to prevent him. The former, drawing his butcher-knife, thrust it at the eyes and nose of his antagonist. Not fancying such *sharp* and *pointed* hints upon a delicate subject, Mr. Bruin caught hold of the hunter's hand, and, as an earnest of deep sensibility, crushed it between his teeth; nor even then relinquishing his gripe. Transferred to the left hand, the knife continued its work, till the sickening beast commenced sliding downward—dragging the poor hunter also to the ground. Both struck at the same time ; but, at that instant the knife of the hunter pierced the heart of his antagonist, and laid him dead at his feet.

The unfortunate man, however, lost two of his fingers in the affray, and his hand was otherwise so much injured that he has never since recovered its use.

While on this theme, we will add another anecdote of an adventure with a grizzly bear, which happened during an expedition among the mountains.

Several years since, an old trapper by the name of Glass, with his companion, while on an excursion, came upon a large grizzly bear.

Bruin, having received the salute of two rifles, as usual, rushed towards his uncivil assailants, who broke from him with all possible despatch. But Glass, stumbling, fell prostrate in his flight, and before he could recover his feet, the infuriated beast was upon him.

Now commenced a death-struggle. The pistols of the hunter were both discharged in quick succession,—the ball of one encering the breast of his antagonist, and that of the other grazing his back.

Smarting and maddened by the pain of additional wounds, the bleeding monster continued the conflict with the fury of desperation,—tearing from the limbs and body of the unfortunate man large pieces of trembling flesh, and lacerating him with the deep thrusts of his teeth and claws.

Meanwhile the sufferer maintained, with his butcher-knife, an obstinate defence, though with fast waning effort and strength. Finally, enfeebled from the loss of blood, and exhausted by the extraordinary exertions of a desperate and unequal contest, he was unable to oppose further resistance, and quietly resigned himself to his fate.

The bear, too, with the thick blood oozing from his numerous wounds, and faint from the many stabs among his veins and sinews, seemed equally in favor of a suspension of hostilities; and, extending himself across the hunter's back, he remained motionless for two hours or more.

But now another enemy commences an assault upon his vitals —that enemy is death. In vain is every defensive effort. In vain are all his struggles. He falls by the hunter's side a lifeless corse.

The setting sun had cast his lurid glare upon the ensanguined spot, as the cowardly comrade of the miserable Glass ventured near to ascertain the result of the fierce and desperate encounter.

There lay the body of his deserted friend, stretched out upon the ground, apparently lifeless, and half-torn to pieces; and, by its side, lay the carcase of that enemy, which had waged with it such murderous war, cold and stiffened in the grasp of death !

Now, doubly terrified at his loneliness, but still governed by sordid motives, he stripped the former of his arms and every other valuable, then no longer needed (as he supposed) by their owner, and, mounting his horse, started immediately for the nearest trading post.

On his arrival he recounted the particulars of the fatal occurrence,—carefully concealing, however, his own criminal conduct. The story was accredited, and the name of Glass found place upon the long catalogue of those who had fallen a prey to wild beasts and savage men.

Six weeks passed, and no one thought of the subject of our

sketch as among the living. The general surprise, therefore, may be readily imagined, on opening the fort-gates one morning, at finding before them the poor, emaciated form of a man, half-naked, and covered with wounds and running sores, and so torn that the fleshless bones of his legs and thighs were exposed to view in places! and how this astonishment was heightened on recognising the person of Glass in the illy defined lineaments of his countenance—the very man so long regarded as an inhabitant of another world! A veritable ghost suddenly appearing upon the spot, could not have occasioned greater wonder!

But, sensations of pity and commiseration quickly succeeded those of surprise, and the unhappy sufferer was taken within doors and received from the hands of friends that careful attention his situation so much required.

The story of his misfortunes was thrillingly interesting. When left by his companion for dead, he was in a state of unconsciousness, with scarcely the breath of life retained in his mangled body. But, the soft night-wind staunched his wounds, and a slight sleep partially revived him from his death-like stupor.

With the morning, the slight sensations of hunger he began to experience were appeased from the raw flesh of the carcase at his side; and, thus strengthened, by a slow and tedious effort he was enabled to reach a near stream and quench his thirst. Still further revived, he again crawled to the carcase at the demands of appetite.

In this manner he continued for three days, when the putrescent corse compelled him to abandon it.

Then it was he commenced his tedious return to the fort, (some seventy miles distant,) which he performed during an interval of forty successive days! The whole of this long stretch he crawled upon his hands and knees,—subsisting, for the meanwhile, only upon insects, such as chance threw in his way, but passing most of the time without one morsel with which to appease the gnawings of hunger or renew his wasted strength.

Yet, great as were his sufferings and intolerable as they may seem, he survived them all, and, by the kind attention of friends, soon recovered.

He still lives in the town of Taos, New Mexico, and frequently relates to wondering listeners the particulars of this terrific and painful adventure.

As this chapter savors somewhat of the *serio-comical*, the reader may be amused with an account of the first nuptial ceremony ever performed in Oregon. This took place on the 20th of July 1813, and the gallant Duncan McDongal of the Pacific Fur Company, was the happy groom on that august occasion, and the daughter of Comcomly, chief of the Chinook tribe of Indians, was the fair bride. In March of the above mentioned year, McDougal visited the north side of the Columbia river, at its mouth, where Comcomly and his people resided in primeval simplicity ; and on his return, a wave broke over his boat, and upset it in a gale. At this important juncture, the one-eyed chief showed himself the white man's friend, and come bounding over the waves in his light canoe, and snatched Mc from a watery grave. He took him back to his village, and hospitably entertained him for three days. During this time, Comcomly made his people perform antics before his redoubtable visitor, and his wives and daughters endeavored by all the endearing and soothing arts of women, to find favor in his eyes. Some of the daughters of his majesty, even painted themselves with red clay, and annointed with fish oil, to give additional *odour* and *lustre* to their charms. Mr. McDougal, though rough and weather-beaten, seems to have had a heart susceptible to the influence of the gentler sex ; but whether it was first trifled with on this occasion, or not, remains in profound uncertainty. Many uncharitable historians are unwilling to award to Mr. McDougal that goodness of heart which first prompted this union ; such, affirm, that it was a *high state alliance*—a *great stroke* of *policy*. They say, tho factory had to depend, in a great measure, on the Chincoks for provisions. They were at present friendly, but it was to be feared they would prove otherwise, should they discover the weakness and exigencies of the post, and the intention to leave the country. This alliance, therefore, would infallibly rivet Comcomly to the interests of the colonists, and with him the powerful tribe of Chinooks. Be this as it may, and it is hard to fathom the real policy of *governors* and *princes*. McDougal despatched two of the clerks as *ambassadors extraordinary*, to wait upon the old chieftain, and make overtures for the heart and hand of his daughter. The Chinooks, though not a very refined nation, were found to have notions of matrimonial etiquette that would not disgrace the most refined sticklers for settlements and pin-money. The suitor repaired, not to the bower of his lady-love, but to her father's lodge, and throws down a present at his feet.

His wishes were then disclosed by some discreet friend employed by him for the purpose. If the suitor and his present found favor in the eyes of the father, he broke the matter to his daughter, and inquired into the state of her inclinations. Should her answer be favorable, the suit was accepted, and the lover was to make further presents to the father, of horses, canoes, and other valuables, according to the beauty and merits of the bride ; looking forward, however, to a return in kind whenever they should go to house-keeping.

Never was the proverbial shrewdness of Comcomly exerted more adroitly than on this occasion. He was a great friend of McDougal, and pleased with the idea of having so distinguished a son-in-law ; but so favorable an opportunity of benefiting his own fortune, was not likely to occur a second time, and he determined to make the most of it. Accordingly, the negotiation was protracted with great diplomatic skill. Conference after conference was held with the two hireling ambassadors : Comcomly was exorbitant in his demands , rating the charms of his daughter at the highest price,and indeed she is represented as having one of the flattest and most aristocratical heads in the tribe. The preliminaries being at length happily adjusted, early in the afternoon of the appointed day, a squadron of canoes crossed from the village of the Chinooks bearing the royal family of Comcomly, and all his court.

That worthy chief landed in princely state, arrayed in a bright blue blanket, with an extra allowance of paint and feathers, and attended by a troop of half naked warriors and nobles. A horse was in waiting to receive the princess, who was mounted behind one of the clerks, on the animal, and thus conveyed, coy but compliant, to the fortress. Here she was received with devout, though decent joy, by her expecting bridegroom.

Her bridal adornments, at first caused some little dismay, having painted and annointed herself for the occasion according to the Chinook toilet ; by dint, however, of copious ablutions, she was freed from all adventitious color and fragrance, and it is said she entered into the nuptial state, the cleanest princess that had ever been known, of the somewhat unctuous tribe of Flat heads.

From that time forward, Comcomly was a daily visiter at the fort, and was admitted into the most intimate councils of his son-in-law.

As we have before stated, the fate of Astoria was consummated by a regular ceremonial, when Captain Black arrived in the

Racoon.   Attended by his officers, the captain entered the fort, and caused the British standard to be erected, broke a bottle of wine, and declared, in a loud voice, that he took possession of the establishment and of the country, in the name of George III, changing the name of Astoria to that of Fort George.   The Chinook warriors, who had offered their services to repel the strangers, were present on this occasion.   McDougal explained it to them as a friendly arrangement, but they shook their heads wisely, considering it an act of subjugation of their ancient allies. They regretted that they had complied with McDougal's wishes, in laying aside their arms, and remarked that, however the A-mericans might conceal the fact, they were undoubtedly all *slaves*; nor could they be persuaded of the contrary, until they beheld the Raccoon depart wihtout tak'nʒ away any prisoners.

As to Comcomly, he never after prided himself upon his *white son-in-law*, but whenever he was asked about him, shook his head mournfully, and replied, that his daughter had perpetrated a great mistake, and, instead of getting a great warrior for a husband, *had married herself to a squaw.*

EMIGRANT ROUTE,

FROM

MISSOURI TO OREGON.

EMIGRANTS to Oregon Territory, cross the Rocky Mountains by the South Pass, a gap of about 20 miles wide. It is at the head of the Sweet Water River, a tributary of the North Fork of the Platte or Nebraska, and in latitude 42° 25′ N., and longitude 109° 10′ W., 950 miles from the mouth of the Kanzas River, and 1174 from the mouth of the Columbia. The following are the distances of the principal points on the route :—

From Westport, Mo., to Kanzas Crossings,	70	American Falls,	22
		Lewis River Crossings,	180
To Platte River,	215	Fort Boise,	128
Forks of Platte River,	115	Burnt River,	114
Chimney Rock,	150	Grand Rond,	30
Scott's Bluff,	20	Fort Wallawalla,	82
Fort Laramie,	60	John Day's River,	112
Red Buttes,	161	Falls River,	21
Rock Independence,	52	Dalls of Columbia,	25
South Pass,	107	Cascades,	36
Green River,	80	Fort Vancouver,	54
Bear River,	130	Oregon City,	16
Fort Hall,	60		

Total from Westport to Oregon City, 2040 miles.

APPENDIX.

Hudson's Bay Company—North-West Company—British Land Expeditions.
Provisions of the Treaties of Utrecht, Versailles, and Ghent, and Convention of St. Petersburgh.

The British Government, which, since the exploration of Hudson's and Baffin's Bays, about the beginning of the sixteenth century, had been anxious to explore the regions lying west of those
waters, as well with the purpose of discovering a water communication between the Atlantic and Pacific Oceans, as of ascertaining its capabilities for commercial pursuits, in 1669, granted the
entire region lying around Hudson's Bay to an association of
London Merchants, called the Hudson's Bay Company, with the
understanding that this Company should endeavor to obtain accurate information on these subjects. Accordingly, in 1769, the
Hudson's Bay Company sent out Mr. Samuel Hearne on an exploring expedition west of Hudson's Bay. In this expedition he
discovered Great Slave Lake and other smaller Lakes, from one
of which a stream issued, flowing towards the north. This river
called the Coppermine, he traced to its termination in a sea,
which he supposed to be the Pacific Ocean, near the 68th parallel of latitude. The information obtained by him, though con
sidered highly important by Great Britain, had no direct connex-
ion with that part of the continent known as the Territory of
Oregon, and is inserted here, only because considered advisable
to give a brief account of the most important expeditions made
by the British, by land.

In the year 1787 the principal fur traders in Canada formed
themselves into an association called the *North West Company*,
and in the course of the next two years extended their operations
as far as Lake Athabasca, near the 59th parallel of latitude, 800
miles beyond Lake Superior, from which point they in 1789 sent
out Mr. Alexander Mackenzie to explore the regions lying farther west. In this journey he discovered a river situated west of
the Coppermine which he called Mackenzie's River.

In a second expedition in 1792-3 he crossed the Rocky Mountains and descended a river called the Tacoutcha, a short distance,

and thence proceeding by land, reached the Pacific, July 22d, 1793, at the mouth of an inlet near the Princess Royal Islands in latitude 52° 20'.

The Tacoutcha was for some time supposed to be a branch of the Columbia, but is the stream now known as Frazer's River, emptying into the Strait of Fuca. Mackenzie's Journal of these two expeditions was published at London in 1802.

The first establishment of the British fur traders beyond the Rocky Mountains was made in 1806, when Mr. Simon Frazer, a Member of the North West Company, established a trading post on Frazer's Lake, near the 54th parallel of latitude, in the country now called New Caledonia. In the year 1811, Mr. Thompson, the astronomer of the North-West Company, hear-.ing of the projected establisnment of a factory at the mouth of the Columbia by Americans, made his way with a party down the northern branch of the Columbia, built a few huts, and opened a trade with the Flat Head and Kootanie Indians, and hastened down to the mouth of the Columbia, only to find the American party already in possession.

The Hudson's Bay and North-West Companies, have ever since their establishment, been at enmity with each other.

This variance, which previous to the year 1814 had only been exhibited by the commission of trifling injuries by each company against the other, in that year, broke out in open war between the rival parties, in the course of which various trading posts were taken and burnt, and in 1816, a battle was fought, between a party of Scotchmen, occupying a post on the Red River, under a grant from the Hudson's Bay Company, and a party belonging to the North-West ompany, in which the Scotchmen were routed, and eighteen of their number killed. These affairs being brought before the British Parliament, in 1822 a compromise was effected between the two rival companies, by which they were united under the name of the Hudson's Bay Company, and by act of Parliament this company received grants for exclusive trade in all the territories north of Canada and the United States, as also in those west of the Rocky Mountains, *and the servants of the company were commissioned to act as Justices of the Peace, so that the jurisdiction of the Courts of Upper Canada was carried to the shores of the Pacific.*

According to the terms of the convention of 1818, British subjects were equally entitled with American citizens to trade in the country west of the Rocky Mountains, which arrangement has proved of immense advantage to the Hudson's Bay Company, which has availed itself of the opportunities thus presented to their fullest extent, and has now become truly powerful in all that region west of the Rocky Mountains. In the words of Mr. Greenhow, " This company is indeed a powerful body, or rather a great power in America. Its posts may be found occupying all the most important points in those regions ; its boats may be met on every stream, conveying British manufactures to the interior, or furs to the great depositories on the sea-board, for shipment to England in British vessels, and the Indians are everywhere so tutored and managed by its agents, that they have been the willing slaves of the Association, and are ready at any time to strike at its adversaries."

The affairs of this company are managed by a Governor, Deputy Governor, and Board of Directors, resident in London, by whom all orders are issued, and to whom all the reports and accounts are rendered.

The officers, superintendents and employees of the company in America, are mostly natives of Great Britain, and the hunters, trappers, *voyageurs*, &c., are principally Indians, half-breeds, and French Canadians. The strictest discipline and subordination are everywhere observed, the country is divided into districts, each of which is under the immediate supervision of an agent, who receives and distributes the goods sent from England, and forwards, the furs collected to the grand depots at Montreal, on the St. Lawrance, York factory, on Hudson's Bay, and Fort Vancouver on the Columbia. From Fort Vancouver the furs are shipped direct to London by ships which arrive annually, bringing merchandise for the trade. They have also a steamboat, and several smaller vessels of from one to three hundred tons burthen, all armed, employed along the coast. The amount of furs obtained by the Company is estimated at about one million of dollars annually, of which one sixth is from the territory west of the Rocky Mountains.

The following extract of a letter from Capt. Spalding, of the Ship Lausanne, of New York, gives still further information in regard to the operations of this Company, so lately as the year 1841.

" The fur trade is entirely monopolized by this Company, but, not content with this, they are turning their attention to every other branch of business. For instance, *they have taken possession of almost every eligible spot in Oregon where there is a wa-*

ter power or a good site for factories, they have erected mills, both saw and flour mills, with the view of supplying the Sandwich Islands with lumber and flour, and the Russians at the north with flour and butter from their farms; *they are, in fact, grasping at everything*, and unless our Government insists on our just rights, and drives them out of the Columbia, they will certainly succeed in driving all the American commerce, both from the Sandwich Islands and California, as they have already done from the North West coast. *Their resourses are immense, and their ambition unbounded.* They annually send a large party through the acknowledged territory of the United States, trap beaver and kill sea-otter. Their trapping party this last year consisted of about seventy men, and they brought in an average quantity of 260 beaver to each man, *all caught within our territory*, say 18,200 beaver worth five dollars each, making the sum total or full value of the skins, ninety-one thousand dollars, *all, or nearly all, taken south of the Columbia and north of California.*

" At present, the Company cultivate about 3000 acres of land, and raise about 18,000 bushels of wheat, 14,000 bushels of potatoes and 3000 bushels of p as. They have a large number of men in their employ, four ships, two schooners and a steamboat. They have several posts on the south side of the Columbia, and take out of the river probably not less than *five hundred thousand dollars per annum*, while our Government remains perfectly passive and unconcerned.

Having given a brief account of the expeditions by sea and land, to the Territory of Oregon, it now remains to offer a succinct account of the treaty stipulations relative to the same country. By the tenth article of Utrecht which was concluded between Great Britain and France in 1713, it was agreed that commissioners should be named to determine within a year " the limits which are to be fixed between the said Bay of Hudson, and the places appertaining to the French," and also "to describe and settle, in like manner, the boundaries between the other British and French colonies, in those parts;" and in conformity with the above article, the said commissioners established the boundary between Canada and Louisiana on the one side, and the Hudson's Bay and North West Companies on the other, by "a line to commence at a cape or promontory on the Ocean in 58° 31' nort , latitude ; to run thence south-westwardly to latitude 49° north from the equator, and along that line *indefinitely* westward." The single word *indefinitely*, the British have endeavored to limit or expunge ever since the discovery of the Columbia by Americans. And why? Simply because if the line of partition were continued to the Pacific Ocean, or "indefinitely" on the 49th parallel, it would cut off Great Britain from the mouth of the Columbia, its harbor, and the rich and timbered region along the banks of that river ; thus rendering the territory comparatively valueless to her. Her aim therefore has been to make that " indefinite" line, definite ; and to check its course at the Rocky Mountains.

By the treaty of Versailles, in 1763, betwen France and Great Britain, the northern boundary of Louisiana is clearly recognised to be a line drawn *due west from the source of the Mississippi, assigning to England, the territory north of the 49th parallel of latitude and east of the Mississippi.*

At that time, Great Britain claimed no other portion of the Continent. In a report, made by Mr. Cushing, to the House of Representatives, Jan. 4th, 1839, (to which the author is endebted for valuable information) we find the following sentence, relative to this subject.

" As between France and Great Britain, or Great Britain and the United States, the successor of all the rights of France, the question of boundary would seem to be concluded by the treaty of Versailles ; in which Great Britain relinquishes, *irrevocably all pretensions west of the Mississippi.*"

In the year 1762, Louisiana, which was originally settled by the French, was ceded to Spain, which nation retained possession of it until 1800, and then retroceded it to France ; " the same in extent, as it now is in the hands of Spain, as it was when France formerly possessed it, and as it should be according to the treaties subsequently made between Spain and other nations.''

On the 30th of April, 1803, Louisiana came into the hands of the United States, by purchase from France, " with all its rights and appurtenances, as fully and in the same manner, as it had been acquired from Spain," in 1800.

By the terms of the convention between the United States and Russia, signed at St. Petersburgh in 1824, it was agreed that thereafter, " there should not be formed by citizens of the United States, any establishment upon the North-West coast of America, to *the north of* 54° 40' of north latitude, and there should none be formed by Russian subjects, *south* of the same parallel.''

By the first article of the treaty of Ghent, which was signed in 1814, by the Plenipotentiaries of the United States and Great

Britain, it was agreed, "that all territory, places, and possessions whatever, taken by either party from the other, during or after the war," (except certain islands in the Atlantic, claimed by both nations,) "should be restored without delay;" and in accordance with the treaty, the settlement at the mouth of the Columbia, called Astoria, and by the British, Fort George, was on the 6th of October, 1818, restored by the British Government, to the U. States, and this restoration of the settlement, was made without any reservation of rights to the country ; as will be shown by the act of delivery, annexed : thus virtually acknowledging the claim of the United States.

"In obedience to the commands of his Royal Highness, the Prince Regent, signified in a despatch from the Right Honorable the Earl Bathurst, addressed to the partners or agents of the North-West Company, bearing date the 27th of January, 1818, and in obedience to a subsequent order, dated the 26th of July, from W. H. Sheriff, Esq., Captain of his Majesty's Ship Andromache, we, the undersigned, do, in conformity to the first article of the Treaty of Ghent, restore to the Government of the United States, through its agent, J. B. Prevost, Esq., the settlement of Fort George, on the Columbia River.

"Given under our hands, in triplicate, a Fort George, (Columbia River,) this 6th day of October, 1818.
(Signed,)

> P. HICKEY, Captain of his Majesty's Ship Blossom.
> J. KEITH, of the North-West Company."

By the third article of the convention of 1818, between the United States and Great Britain, "it is agreed that any country that may be claimed by either party on the North-West coast of America, westward of the Stoney Mountains, shall, together with its harbors, bays and creeks, and the navigation of all rivers within the same, be free and open for the term of ten years from the date of the signature of the present convention, to the vessels, citizens and subjects of the two Powers; it being well understood, that this agreement is not to be construed to the prejudice of any claim, which either of the two high contracting parties may have, to any part of the said country."

By the first article of the convention of 1827, it was agreed by the United States and Great Britain, that the provisions of the third article of the convention of 1818, should be "indefinitely extended and continued in force in the same manner as if all the provisions of the said article were herein specifically stated."

By the second article of the same convention, it was agreed that either party might, "on giving due notice of twelve months to the other contracting party, annul and abrogate this convention ; and it shall in such case be accordingly annulled and abrogated, after the expiration of the said term of notice."

In the articles of these conventions, it should be distinctly noticed, that no reference whatever is made to the possession ; which was in the most formal manner, acknowledged by the delivery of Astoria to the United States, under the provisions of the Treaty of Ghent, previously noticed, to be vested in the United States.

According to the established laws of nations, the title to the Oregon Territory depends upon the first discovery and occupancy, and upon purchase and cessions by treaty, from the first discoverer or occupant.

In the preceding pages, it is clearly shown that the Spaniards first discovered and surveyed the coast, that the Columbia was first seen and entered by Captain Gray, an American navigator, who gave it the name of his own ship—that an American party, under Messrs. Lewis and Clarke, first explored the Columbia from its source to its mouth, where they built Fort Clatsop ; and spent the winter of 1805–6 there. That the Pacific or American Fur Company, at the head of which was Mr. Astor, a merchant of New York, formed the first permanent settlement at the mouth of the Columbia, and along the Columbia River. That this settlement was taken possession of by the British, during the war, *and subsequently restored to the United States Government, under the provisions of the Treaty of Ghent, without any reservation of the right of sovereignty*; that by the Treaty of Utrecht, Great Britain relinquished irrevocably all title to the country south of the 49th parallel, in favor of France, and by the treaty of 1803, between the United States and France, the United States became successor to France, in that part of her dominions, and by treaty with Spain, subsequently ratified and acknowledged by Mexico, the United States became possessed of all the rights of Spain west of the Rocky Mountains, and north of the 42d parallel.

Such has ever been the nature of our title to Oregon—such the positions upon which we have ever founded our claim to the whole of the rich country watered by the Colubia ; and almost any one of these positions, would be sufficient to establish our claim against that of any and every other nation.

The discovery of a territory, and actual possession of it, is uni-

versally acknowledged to give the right to form settlements throgh-
out the same ; so also, the discovery of a river and taking possession of a post upon it, within a reasonable time, give the right
to form settlements in every portion of the territory drained by
such river, or its tributaries.

That the United States Government has obtained such a right
to the Territory of Oregon, is abundantly proved—and this right
has never been relinquished, nor forfeited by *non user*. That
we took possession within a reasonable time, is admitted on all
hands. Our post on the Columbia, was taken possession of by the
British in time of open war—and after the concluding of peace,
was restored to the United States Government, without reservation ; and by the terms of the convention of 1818, by which British subjects were allowed to hunt, fish, and trade in the territory,
it was declared that no portion of that agreement should be construed to the prejudice of any claim which either party had to
the country.

Index

COLOPHON

The Herman Leonard **HISTORY OF THE OREGON TERRITORY** was printed in the workshop of Glen Adams, which is located in the quiet country village of Fairfield, southern Spokane County, in Washington State. Reproduced sheets of the original 134 year old pages were photographed with some enlargedment. Type for the index was set in ten point Baskerville roman and italic by Miss Angela Wolf, using a Compugraphic 48 computer photosetter. The introduction was set by Glen Adams, who also handset and printed the title page. The index was made up by Edward J. Kowrach. Camera-darkroom work was by Evelyn Foote Clausen. The text pages were printed by Ralph Decker using a 770CD Hamada offset press. The stripping was also done by Ralph Decker. Folding and assembly work is by Evelyn Foote Clausen and Miss Angela Wolf. The paper stock is eighty pound Lowell. Binding is by William Bosch of Oakesdale, Washington.

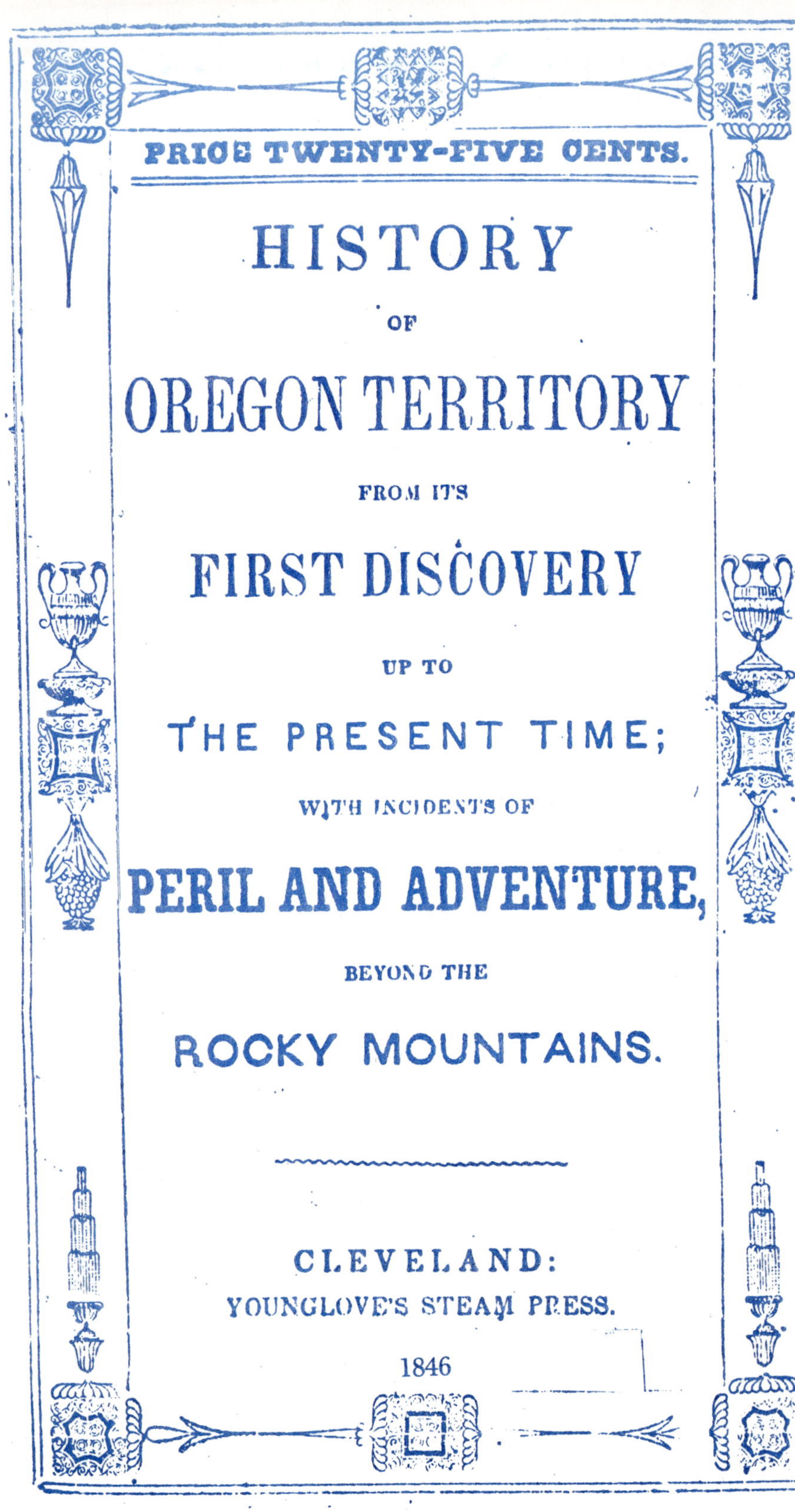

HISTORY

OF

OREGON TERRITORY

FROM ITS

FIRST DISCOVERY

UP TO

THE PRESENT TIME;

WITH INCIDENTS OF

PERIL AND ADVENTURE,

BEYOND THE

ROCKY MOUNTAINS.

CLEVELAND:

YOUNGLOVE'S STEAM PRESS.

1846